IMAGES OF WA

THE BATTLE FOR KHARKOV 1941–1943

If this German casualty was lucky, he had bought himself a ticket home, otherwise it was off to a field hospital to be patched up and then back to the front.

IMAGES OF WAR

THE BATTLE FOR KHARKOV 1941–1943

RARE PHOTOGRAPHS FROM WARTIME ARCHIVES

Anthony Tucker-Jones

Pen & Sword
MILITARY

First published in Great Britain in 2016 by
PEN & SWORD MILITARY
an imprint of
Pen & Sword Books Ltd,
47 Church Street,
Barnsley,
South Yorkshire
S70 2AS

A CIP record for this book is available from the British Library.

ISBN 978 1 47382 747 9

Typeset by CHIC GRAPHICS

Printed and bound by CPI Group (UK) Ltd, Croydon, CR0 4YY

Pen & Sword Books Ltd incorporates the imprints of Pen & Sword Archaeology,
Atlas, Aviation, Battleground, Discovery, Family History, History, Maritime, Military,
Naval, Politics, Railways, Select, Social History, Transport, True Crime, Claymore
Press, Frontline Books, Leo Cooper, Praetorian Press, Remember When, Seaforth
Publishing and Wharncliffe.

For a complete list of Pen & Sword titles please contact
Pen & Sword Books Limited
47 Church Street, Barnsley, South Yorkshire, S70 2AS, England
E-mail: enquiries@pen-and-sword.co.uk
Website: www.pen-and-sword.co.uk

Contents

Introduction

Ukraine's capital Kiev and its second city Kharkov proved to be major battlegrounds during the bloody campaigns fought on the Eastern Front during 1941–1945. Kharkov was the scene of four critical battles during the Second World War. Crucially, in the aftermath of the initial success of Adolf Hitler's Operation Barbarossa, the Wehrmacht was not quick enough to prevent the relocation of Kharkov's vital armaments factories, including a key tank factory. The city was the birthplace of the Red Army's T-34 medium tank, which ultimately would give it a much-needed edge over Hitler's panzers.

At the outbreak of war Kharkov was swiftly captured following the Red Army's defeat at Kiev and subsequent withdrawal. A second battle occurred when the Red Army launched a disastrous counteroffensive in the spring of 1942. The third engagement occurred in early 1943 when the Red Army launched a second counteroffensive that was similarly crushed after Field Marshal von Manstein conducted a brilliant tactical withdrawal only to reoccupy Kharkov. The fourth battle finally saw the city liberated once and for all by an operation launched in the wake of Hitler's catastrophic defeat at Kursk in the summer of 1943. Such was the Wehrmacht's waning power that it could no longer hold Ukraine's second city and the fighting moved ever westward.

Despite its strategic significance, Kharkov never loomed large in Hitler's planning for the invasion of the Soviet Union and the defeat of Stalin's Red Army. Moscow and Leningrad were always seen as the competing prizes, followed by the Caucasian oilfields. Major General Erich Marcks, working under the auspices of General Halder, the German Army Chief of Staff, envisaged allocating the bulk of the German forces to an army group that would strike east across occupied Poland to Moscow via Minsk and Smolensk, while another group attacked southeastwards towards Kiev.

Marcks advocated subsidiary flanking operations conducted against Leningrad and a southern advance against Kiev by German–Romanian forces striking from annexed Bessarabia. The central army group's objectives of Moscow and Kiev were the key, which would ensure the Red Army was trapped and destroyed between the Dvina and Dnieper in nine to seventeen weeks.

In fairness, the Marcks' plan was just that: a planning study rather than a fully fledged operational plan. However, it laid down the fundamental strategy for Operation Barbarossa, though it was to be much amended and Hitler's and the

Army's strategic views were to diverge considerably. Most notably, Hitler would see the capture of Leningrad not as a third primary objective, as advocated by the Army, but as an essential factor before the crucial drive on Moscow.

Marcks assumed that although the Wehrmacht would have only a small advantage in men, it would make up for this with a distinct superiority in armoured units and quality of equipment. European occupation forces aside, Marcks calculated that the Germans could muster 110 infantry divisions, 24 panzer divisions and 12 motorised divisions against 96 Soviet rifle divisions, 23 cavalry divisions and 28 armoured brigades. He was unaware, however, that Marshal Timoshenko was resurrecting the Red Army's tank divisions and mechanised corps.

When Marcks presented his 'Operational Draft East' for the Army High Command or Oberkommando des Heeres (OKH), it was with Halder's approval that he made Moscow the key objective. The Red Army would be drawn to the Soviet capital and destroyed on the road to Moscow. Subsidiary operations in the south would protect Romania's oilfields and pre-empt any Soviet counterattacks. Once Moscow had been captured, the Wehrmacht could then swing south to crush the remains of the Red Army in Ukraine – only then would Kiev, and to a lesser extent Kharkov, attain any real strategic importance.

This meant Byelorussia or White Russia and not Ukraine would be the main battlefield and Marcks called for 70 per cent of the German armour to be massed north of the vast Pripet Marshes. A winter campaign was not considered because it was anticipated that the Red Army would have collapsed by then. Field Marshal von Brauchitsch, the Army's Commander-in-Chief, and Halder, the Chief of Staff, agreed that the main weight of their attack should fall along the Minsk–Smolensk–Moscow land bridge. This would be the dagger thrust to the heart of the Red Army.

In October 1940 Halder's staff estimated they would be facing 170 Soviet divisions; in fact, although they believed this to be an overestimate, it was actually too low. Lieutenant Colonel Bernard von Lossberg produced his 'Build-up East' (*Aufbau Ost*) plan for the armed forces' High Command Oberkommando der Wehrmacht (OKW), which laid greater emphasis on the flanks. Nonetheless, the operational plan presented to Field Marshal Alfred Jodl, Chief of the OKW Staff, on 19 September 1940 saw the main blow falling north of the Pripet Marshes for a push towards Moscow.

Hitler chose to ignore the lessons drawn from a war game directed by General Paulus between 28 November and 3 December 1940, concluding that Moscow was not that important. His eye was drawn to protecting Romania's oilfields and securing Ukraine's raw materials, which inevitably meant the key effort would have to be in the south. The deployment directive (*Aufmarschweisung*) Barbarossa, issued on 31 January 1941, added Romania to the area of responsibility of Field Marshal von

Rundstedt's Army Group South. Nowhere, though, did Kharkov figure in any of these detailed deliberations.

Ironically, the city was to become the focal point for a number of Soviet counteroffensives that would ultimately unhinge the Wehrmacht's position in Ukraine and the Crimea. It was Hitler's failure to cut off the Soviets' Kursk salient that ensured Kharkov's eventual deliverance.

Photograph Sources

All the images in this book are courtesy of the Scott Pick *WWII Russian Front Original Photo Collection*. This consists of almost 2,500 black and white photographs providing a remarkable and often grim insight into many aspects of the war on the Eastern Front. Notably, the quality of the photos is consistently high throughout the archive. Most of those selected by the author to illustrate this title have never been published before. Pen & Sword and the author are indebted to Scott Pick for his generous assistance with this project.

Chapter One

Kharkov: City of the Tractor

In 1941 Kharkov was one of the Soviet Union's most important strategic centres due to its vital military factories and its railway and airline links. It was not only a vital communications hub for the whole of Ukraine, but also connected the Crimea, Caucasus, Dnieper and Donbas regions. The Caucasus held vital oilfields, while the Donets was rich in coal. All of these were obvious targets following Hitler's invasion of the Soviet Union in June 1941.

The city was host to one of the most important tank factories in the country and was where Mikhail Koshkin's brand new T-34 tank was being built. Hitler was oblivious to the development of the T-34 and it was to be an intelligence blunder that would cost him dearly. The failure to capture the T-34 factory at Kharkov before it escaped was to prove another strategic blunder. In addition to the vital Kharkov tractor and locomotive plants, the city was also host to the Kharkov Aircraft Plant and the Turbine Plant. These were churning out a plethora of military products, including tanks, fighter aircraft, military tractors, mortars, small arms and ammunition.

Most notably, Kharkov was home to the BT-5 and BT-7 fast tanks and the T-35 heavy tank, which went into production there in the 1930s. It was also involved with the building of the T-26 light tank. The BTs and the T-26 formed the backbone of the Red Army's tank fleet in 1941, although they had already been proved obsolete during the Spanish Civil War and the Finnish Winter War. Mikhail Koshkin was appointed head of the Kharkov design bureau in the mid-1930s to work on BT improvements; this led to the development of the T-34, which went into production in 1940.

As well as tanks, Kharkov also manufactured tractors or tracked prime movers. Ukraine was the breadbasket of the Soviet Union so these tractors were invaluable to Ukrainian agriculture. The first Soviet trucks and cars appeared in the 1920s, coming out of Moscow's AMO and Spartak factories respectively. GAZ, with the assistance of American Ford technicians, then set up a factory at Gorky in the early 1930s. Tractor and truck production also started in the early 1930s with civilian and military tracked tractors being built in Chelyabinsk, Kharkov, Kirov and Stalingrad. All of the Red Army's heavy artillery was hauled by full-tracked prime movers. Those produced at Kharkov's Komintern factory were used to tow the 152mm gun howitzer M1937.

The Kharkov Aircraft Plant was home to Pavel Sukhoi's design bureau until its move to Molotov in 1941. His Su-2 short-range bomber went into production in 1939 at Kharkov's Factory No.135 and by September 1941 this was producing five aircraft a day. This factory was relocated in the face of the German advance, and the aircraft was also constructed in Moscow and Taganrog.

While Hitler's main objectives before the winter of 1941 focused on the seizure of Leningrad, Moscow and the approaches to the Caucasian oilfields, Kharkov was clearly a key secondary objective. The German high command appreciated the value of the city as a vital rail hub and industrial centre that should be denied the Soviets. The capture of Kharkov would mean that the Red Army's Southwestern and Southern Fronts would have to rely on Voronezh and Stalingrad as their transport centres.

Despite his ignorance of the T-34, Hitler was well aware of Kharkov's military significance: 'The second in importance is south Russia, particularly the Donets Basin, ranging from the Kharkov region. There is the whole basis of [the] Russian economy; if the area is mastered then it would inevitably lead to the collapse of the entire Russian economy . . .' Hitler's assessment was right but delays in securing Kharkov meant that its factories slipped from his grasp.

Following the German invasion, the T-34 was swiftly forced from its birthplace. Fortunately for the Red Army, the Kharkov locomotive factory began to relocate to Nizhny Tagil in August 1941. Following the successful relocation of the Soviet tank-producing facilities east of the Urals during 1941, production of the T-34 was successfully conducted at Chelyabinsk and Nizhny Tagil, as well as at a number of other subsidiary plants well out of the reach of the Luftwaffe.

While Kharkov is principally remembered as the birthplace of the famous T-34 tank, it is equally famous for its enormous Dzerzhinsky Square, which was photographed on numerous occasions during the war by both sides. The Square is bordered by massive and oppressive Stalinist tower blocks that are a fine example of totalitarian and utilitarian architecture. Perversely, the square was named after Felix Dzerzhinsky, the founder of the Cheka – the Bolshevik police (and forerunners of the KGB). During the course of the fighting it was renamed by its conquerors 'German Army Square' and then 'Leibstandarte SS Square'.

In the spring of 1941 the population of Kharkov numbered just under a million, but once the Nazi invasion commenced the city became jammed with evacuees and refugees fleeing the fighting. Ironically, Hitler's invasion helped concentrate Soviet weapons manufacture. For example, at the outbreak of war T-34 production was in fact far from centralised and was spread over vast distances. Leningrad's Kirov

Factory manufactured the L-11 anti-tank gun while electrical components were made at the Dynamo Factory in Moscow. The tanks themselves were initially built in 1940 in Kharkov but numbers were supplemented by production at the Stalingrad Tractor Factory (STZ) in early 1941, then in the middle of that year the Krasnoye Sormovo Factory No.112 in Gorky also began to build T-34s.

The evacuation of Kharkov's factories commenced before Hitler had a chance to attack. Three days before the German assault began on the city on 23 October, seventy factories were stripped and shipped east on 320 trains. The tank factory evacuated to Nizhny Tagil and helped create the Ural Tank Factory No.183. Kharkov's diesel engine factory and Leningrad's Kirov Plant (Factory No.100) and S.M. Kirov (No.185) moved to Chelyabinsk and combined with the Tractor Plant to became popularly known as 'Tankograd' or 'Tank City'. In Molotov the Su-2 bomber was built from the component stock evacuated from Kharkov until late April 1942.

Defeated Soviet troops being escorted to the rear. They are wearing a mixture of the *telogreika* or wadded coat in the front rank and the *Kaftan* or greatcoat. In the face of Barbarossa the Red Army lost tens of thousands of casualties and millions of men captured as its forces were trapped in numerous pockets.

At the beginning of Hitler's Operation Barbarossa the Red Army was driven from eastern Poland and back across Byelorussia and Ukraine with great loss. The rapid collapse of Stalin's so-called 'forward defence' exposed the Soviet Union's cities.

This photograph shows hostile and apprehensive-looking Red Army prisoners captured in the summer of 1941. Just before the outbreak of war the Soviets sought to remove the last Tsarist influences from the Red Army's uniform. This comprised a khaki cotton shirt or *rubaha* seen here with stand-and-fall collar (piped in service colour for officers) and breast patch pockets with a buttoned flap. Sleeves were gathered at the wrist and cuff (piped in arm colour for officers), fastened with two small buttons. It was worn with matching khaki breeches by all ranks except for mounted units who wore royal blue. The *French* or single-breasted tunic, with stand-and-fall collar, six buttons, pleated breast patch pockets with buttoned flaps and side slash pockets with flap, was introduced for officers.

The man in the middle is wearing the *furashka* or peak cap, which had a khaki top and band with piping in arm or service colour. Peak and chin strap were black, and a five-pointed red star was worn in front of the band.

An array of captured Soviet anti-tank guns, heavy and light machine guns and mortars. In the face of such losses it became imperative that the Red Army's factories were saved to help rebuild Stalin's shattered military.

The smashed remains of Soviet T-26 light tanks. Many Soviet tanks went into action with insufficient ammunition and fuel, and in addition the crews were often poorly trained. Components for the T-26 were built in Kharkov.

More knocked-out Soviet T-26 tanks. The Red Army's desperate counterattacks against Hitler's Blitzkrieg could not save the Soviet Union's major cities from occupation and resulted in huge pockets of trapped Soviet troops.

The destruction of the Soviet armies around the Ukrainian capital Kiev in September 1941 sealed the fate of Kharkov. It is unclear why this Ukrainian civilian is amongst the PoWs, but presumably the Germans rounded up all males of fighting age in the vicinity.

Minsk, the capital of Byelorussia, fell in late June 1941. Statues of Lenin dominated the Soviet Union's cities as much as Stalin. This particular one stood before Minsk's 'House of Soviets' before the SS brought it crashing down. The Germans were swift to vandalise the symbols of Bolshevism and loot museums and galleries. When fighting for the Minsk pocket ceased in early July 1941, the Germans claimed 342,000 prisoners of war, 3,332 tanks and 1,809 guns destroyed or captured. This left Smolensk, Kiev and Kharkov firmly in the firing line.

An upside-down KV-2 on the outskirts of Kharkov. In principle, this heavy breakthrough tank was a promising design, but in practice it failed to live up to expectations.

Picturesque Kharkov sits on the junction of the Kharkov, Lopan and Udy rivers where they flow into the Seversky Donets watershed. The city was a cultural centre as well as an industrial powerhouse. The bell tower of Assumption Cathedral, which the Soviets closed in 1929, is clearly visible in the background.

The northwestern half of the massive modernist Dzerzhinsky Square, which is reputed to be the eighth largest square in Europe.

Located in Dzerzhinsky Square, Kharkov's very distinctive Derzhprom building, completed in 1928, was also known as the State Industry Building or the Palace of Industry. This modernist architecture designed by the Constructivist school was later denounced by Stalinist architects.

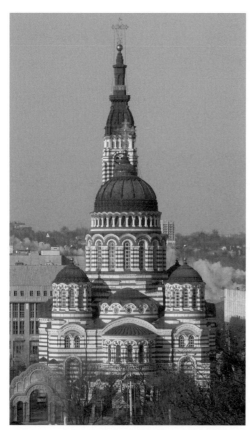

Kharkov's Annunciation Cathedral was completed in 1888. It was closed to worshippers in 1930 but German occupation forces reopened it in 1943.

All of the Soviet Union's civic buildings were dominated by modernist architecture. Note the 'Hammer and Sickle' on this building being used as a German HQ.

Once the fighting started, many of the historic and centuries-old buildings in Kharkov, Kiev, Minsk, Smolensk and elsewhere were damaged or destroyed beyond repair.

The fine icons of this Russian Orthodox Church lie exposed following heavy bombardment. Both sides tended to use such structures as strongpoints and for artillery spotting and they inevitably drew enemy fire.

The Red Army takes centre stage, along with Stalin and Lenin, on this military HQ building or training school. Note the statue of the tanker on the right (identifiable by the one-piece overall and padded helmet). Soviet tank forces proved a shambles in the face of Hitler's Blitzkrieg.

More damaged Russian or Ukrainian places of worship; in reality, many had already fallen into disrepair under Soviet rule.

Chapter Two

Stalin's Soviet 38th Army

The Soviet 6th Army was reactivated in August 1939 in the Kiev Special Military District. It was involved in the invasion of eastern Poland in September 1939, and then occupied defences along the Lvov axis as a premier military district 'covering army'. Under Lieutenant General I.N. Muzychenko, the 6th bore the brunt of the main German attack in June 1941, falling back to Uman, south of Kiev, where it was trapped and destroyed along with the 12th Army. Muzychenko was captured and his command was deactivated on 10 August, only to be reactivated the following month around the nucleus of the 48th Rifle Corps and deployed in reserve in the Kharkov sector.

The 21st Army had formed in the spring of 1941 at Kuibyshev in the Volga Military District. In July 1941, with the panzers approaching the Dnieper, it deployed to the Rogachev area and during the next three weeks launched a series of desperate counterattacks against Guderian's 2nd Panzer Group (the infamous 'Timoshenko counteroffensive'). During the fighting in September the 21st Army was destroyed in the Kiev pocket.

The Soviet 38th Army, under Lieutenant General Dimitrii Riabyshev, came into being in early August 1941 just after the destruction of the 6th and 12th Armies at Uman in western Ukraine. Based on 8th Mechanised Corps survivors from the Uman pocket and newly raised Ukrainian divisions, it formed part of the Southwestern Front and was tasked with holding the Dnieper upriver from Kremenchug. After the surrender on 1 August of those forces trapped at Uman, this task was given greater urgency.

At the end of the month Riabyshev was sent south to a new appointment and Major General Nikolai Feklenko assumed command of the 38th Army, which on 31 August found itself resisting the German 17th Army's crossing of the Dnieper. This German bridgehead was to form the southern arm of a pincer designed to trap much of the Southwestern Front east of the river. The northern arm crossed the Desna 125 miles northeast of Kiev.

Feklenko was ordered to destroy the German Dnieper bridgehead but was in no position to do so, especially once panzer divisions from the 1st Panzer Group had crossed the river. The panzers broke through the 38th Army's lines on 12 September and four days later linked up with German armour moving south from Romny. As intended, this trapped most of the Soviet Southwestern Front, including much of the 38th Army. Feklenko was replaced by Major General Vladimir Tsiganov. He was reinforced by reserve units from eastern Ukraine to try to stop the remnants of his army being driven back towards Poltava.

The Red Army's defeat at Kiev was even bigger than that at Uman. When the battle of Kiev came to a close on 26 September 1941, the German official news service claimed that the pocket had given up 665,000 men killed or captured, and no fewer than 884 tanks and 3,718 field guns and mortars captured or destroyed. Staggeringly, five Soviet armies (the 5th, 21st, 26th, 37th and 38th), amounting to fifty field divisions, had been wiped off the Red Army's order of battle. Subsequently the Soviets contested these figures, claiming they lost no more than 175,000 men. The general feeling is that Moscow was trying to play down the situation, while the Germans over-inflated their victory. It seems Stalin remained content to leave these vast forces to their fate, despite the efforts of Military Commissar Nikita Khrushchev and General Semyon Mikhailovich Budenny to save them. When Stalin did relent, it was too late and thousands were killed trying to escape.

Thanks to the German victory at Kiev, the Soviet Southwestern Front was smashed. The Soviet high command dispatched reinforcements into the region between Kursk and Rostov in an attempt to stabilise the southern flank. With the reformed 6th, 21st, 38th and 40th Armies, the front was reconstituted under Marshal Timoshenko. This, though, ended in failure in October when the Germans renewed their attacks. The 6th Army under Rodion Malinovsky and the 38th Army commanded by Tsiganov were driven back after failing to coordinate their efforts. The situation at Vyazma and Bryansk meant that there were no reserves left, forcing Timoshenko to retreat.

At the beginning of October the 38th Army comprised six rifle divisions and a tank division, all being forced back towards Poltava. When the advancing German armoured units were directed towards Moscow and Rostov, Tsiganov was able to avoid being encircled by the German 6th Army's plodding infantry divisions. The 21st Army's supporting 10th Tank Brigade fought alongside the 169th, 300th and 304th Rifle Divisions of the 38th Army in the bitter fighting around Poltava and Kharkov in September and October 1941. It lost its twenty tanks in September and was refitted in early October.

The Ukrainian 169th Rifle Division was formed in the Ukraine Military District (in the Kherson and Nikolaev region) in the summer of 1939. It took part in the invasions of eastern Poland and Romanian Bessarabia. At the time of Hitler's attack on the Soviet Union the 169th was with the 55th Rifle Corps, which was acting as the Kiev Special Military District's reserve. It fought with the 18th Army during the fighting withdrawal across southern Ukraine. Retreating eastwards, it participated first in the 6th Army's defence of the Dnieper river line and then joined the 38th and 21st Armies defending the Kharkov sector. Major General S.M. Rogachevsky was appointed divisional commander on 3 October during the heavy fighting on the approaches to Kharkov.

The Ukrainian 300th and 304th Rifle Divisions were both severely weakened by the ferocity of the autumn operations. By November their combined manpower was less than 2,680 men. Raised at Krasnograd south of Kharkov in July 1941, the 300th initially formed part of the Western Strategic Directions Reserve. The following month it was at Poltava and joined the 38th Army's defence of the Dnieper line south of Kiev. Subsequently it fought with the 38th Army both in defence of Kharkov and during the winter battles that followed. Likewise, the 304th was raised near Kharkov at Solotnoscha in July 1941 using veterans and reservists from the disbanded 109th Motorised Division of the 5th Mechanised Corps that had been mauled in the battles at Lepel and around Smolensk.

The Soviet 38th Army was instructed to hold Kharkov while the city's vital military factories were dismantled and taken to safety. In reality, the 38th Army was more concerned with conducting an orderly withdrawal, so it was really a case of simply buying time until the evacuation had been completed. This job fell to the 216th Rifle Division, reformed after its destruction at Kiev. Formed in May 1941 at Staro Konstantinov in the Kiev Special Military District as a motorised division with the 24th Mechanised Corps, the Ukrainian 216th Rifle Division was deployed south of Kiev at Proskurov when the war started. During July and August it fought with the 24th Corps in the Vinnitsa region and was trapped with the 26th Army at Uman in late August. The 216th was reformed around the division's survivors and served with the 38th Army during the defensive battles on the approaches to Kharkov and Kupiansk.

As the 216th Rifle Division was conducting a holding action, it was offered no support from any of the 38th Army's other divisions, nor indeed from the higher command formations. The 216th moved to defend the western edge of the city, setting up machine-gun nests and mortar pits protected by minefields. It was evident that the first battle for Kharkov was going to be a very brief and one-sided affair. Forced to abandon the city, the 38th Army later joined the Southwestern Front's January offensive towards Kharkov and in March 1942 seized the Staryi Saltov bridgehead just east of the city.

Lieutenant General Krill Semenovich Moskalenko was appointed commander of the 38th Army in March 1942, by this time it consisted of six rifle divisions and three tank brigades. The 36th Tank Brigade, commanded by Colonel T.I. Tanaschisin, formed at Gorky in the Moscow Military District in November 1941 and joined the 38th Army shortly after its creation. The 13th and 133rd Tank Brigades had been formed in the summer of 1941 and had already seen action with the armies of the Southwestern Front.

When the Germans first invaded, Moskalenko, then a brigade commander, tangled with the 1st Panzer Group. After his force was destroyed, he took charge first of the 15th Rifle Corps, then of the 6th Cavalry Corps and a cavalry mechanised group in fighting near Kiev, Chernigov and Elets. For his performance at Elets in late December 1941 he was promoted deputy commander of the 6th Army, then attacking towards Kharkov. Moskalenko played a vital role in planning the 6th Army's role in the Barvenkovo–Lozovaya operation in January 1942, and as a reward was given command of the 38th Army.

The pilot of this Polikarpov I-16 made a wheels-up landing but it's unclear if he survived it. Only in experienced hands was this aircraft a manoeuvrable and worthy opponent for the Luftwaffe, and Stalin had few of these. The Polikarpov I-153 and I-16, along with the MiG-3, formed the mainstay of the Red Air Force's fighter squadrons but they were simply no match for the Luftwaffe's fighters.

Another wrecked Polikarpov I-16, perhaps the result of another crash landing. By 1940 more than 6,500 examples of this little fighter had been built. Unfortunately for newly trained pilots, it was difficult to fly and land.

At least a dozen wrecked aircraft. The Polikarpov I-153 biplane appeared in the late 1930s, but its speed was woefully insufficient against the newer monoplanes entering service in Europe. At 03.15 on 22 June 1941 the Luftwaffe attacked sixty-six Red Air Force airfields – and by noon Stalin had lost 1,200 aircraft. This left the Red Army at the mercy of the Luftwaffe.

Hitler's Blitzkrieg into Ukraine simply outmanoeuvred the Red Army. As a result, huge numbers of troops were captured in the Uman and Kiev pockets. This prisoner is wearing the old civil war era *budenovka* cloth helmet (named after Marshal Budenny). It was phased out from the mid-1930s onwards but was still in use in 1941.

As a prelude to the Red Army's defeats at Kiev and Kharkov, its 6th and 12th Armies were trapped and destroyed at Uman in western Ukraine, losing well over 200,000 men. The Red Army drew recruits from all the ethnic groups who formed part of the Soviet Union, including this Central Asian soldier.

Pensive-looking Red Army officers confer with their German captors. Once encircled, many had no option but to surrender. They are wearing the double-breasted *kaftan* or greatcoat, which was made of dark grey cloth that had a tendency to turn brown.

More Soviet prisoners being escorted to the rear. After the Red Army's defeat at Uman, the Soviets lost five armies and half a million men trapped in the Kiev pocket, leaving the road to Kharkov all but open. Most of the existing rifle units were wiped out during Operation Barbarossa. Although 286 new divisions (including at least 42 'national' divisions, 24 People's Volunteer Divisions and 22 divisions culled from other services) were formed between June and December 1941, manpower shortages meant that divisional strength fell to 10,859.

In the opening stages of the German invasion the Soviet T-35 heavy tank built in Kharkov proved little threat to the panzers. Its large size and inadequate steering made it difficult to manoeuvre and therefore vulnerable.

Just over sixty of these monsters were built between 1933 and 1939. The design had been intended for mass production in Kharkov, but poor quality control scuppered the plan. In addition, the T-35 cost as much as nine BT fast tanks, so the Kharkov factories concentrated on the more versatile BT models.

German troops queue next to an abandoned T-35. It appears to be one of the final batch of six produced in 1938 which received turrets with sloped armour for better protection. It did them little good and they were dumped by their crews as the panzers approached.

At the time of the invasion the Soviet KV-1 and KV-2 heavy tanks were just coming into service. Nicknamed the 'Dreadnought', the KV-2 was largely invulnerable to direct fire from all but high velocity weapons at close range. Nevertheless its wheels and tracks were vulnerable and, once immobilised, the KV was a sitting duck. These tanks were only really effective as static weapons.

Germans examining a 'brewed up' T-26 light tank, which in this instance burned along with its unfortunate crew. This type of tank was built in Leningrad and Stalingrad. During the month-long battle for Ukraine's capital Kiev, the Red Army lost 884 tanks.

This Soviet tanker failed to escape from his T-26 before it brewed up.

Soviet BT-7 fast tanks abandoned at the roadside. Some 5,000 of these were built at the Kharkov Locomotive Factory, along with the T-34 medium tank. After 1941 it was phased out in favour of the T-34.

An abandoned BM-13 Soviet rocket launcher, with an unfired rocket still on its rails.

A Soviet truck mounting heavy machine guns used in an anti-aircraft role. The first dedicated mount for anti-aircraft machine guns, known as a ZPU, went into service in 1931 and was capable of taking up to four M1910 Maxim guns.

A Russian Maxim machine gun used in an anti-aircraft role. During the early stages of the war, Soviet air defences were woefully inadequate. The Russian Maxim M1910, based on Hiram Maxim's machine gun of the same name, was adopted by the Russian Imperial Army in 1910. It was mounted on three slightly differing types of wheeled mount (Sokolov, Kolesnikov and Vladimirov – the later came into service with the Soviets and was known as the 1910/30). It took a 7.62 x 54mm round and had a rate of fire of 600 rounds a minute.

During the battle for Kiev the Red Army lost 3,718 field guns and mortars.

A German column passes Soviet graves marked by an M1910 Maxim heavy machine gun. The road to Kharkov was lined by thousands of such graves. It is noticeable that the weapon's muzzle has been damaged.

Soviet soldiers gunned down in the open. The summer battles of 1941 proved a complete disaster for the Red Army, with entire armies being wiped off its order of battle. The 38th Army was formed from survivors from the Uman pocket.

Soviet Mosin Nagant rifles mark the fallen. At the beginning of the Second World War the 7.62 × 54mm Mosin-Nagant 91/30 was the standard issue rifle of the Red Army. It initially appeared in 1891 but went through numerous modifications. A shortened carbine version known as the M38 also came into service in 1938, followed by the M44. The rifle had a range of 500m but this could be extended to over 800m using sniper sights.

Chapter Three

Hitler's Army Group South

itler's Operation Barbarossa began at 3am on 22 June 1941 and threw 140 divisions with 3,300 panzers, 7,100 guns and 2,770 aircraft at the Soviet Union. Army Group Centre's key role was to charge through Minsk, Orsha and Smolensk and on to Moscow. Within a week the armies of Leeb, Bock and Rundstedt were deep within the Soviet Union and Guderian's panzer spearhead had penetrated almost 300 miles.

At the end of July 1941, after more than five weeks of continuous and bitter fighting, Army Group Centre, whose commander, Field Marshal von Bock, already saw himself as the conqueror of Moscow, paused for breath. Hitler began to cast his eye south and north for the spoils of war. Ukraine, the granary of the Soviet Union, the coal mines and factories of the Donets basin and all the treasures of Leningrad began to call to him.

As a result, once Operation Barbarossa was under way, Hitler issued Führer Directive 34, which reflected his intentions to secure the Leningrad area and the Caucasus before capturing Moscow. Army Group South was tasked with destroying those Red Army forces west of the Dnieper, key amongst them the 5th Soviet Army northwest of Kiev.

Hitler dispatched Army Group Centre's panzers to the flanks, moving them against Leningrad – a region that was simply not good for tank warfare – and into Ukraine. Kiev, though, was not Moscow, that epicentre of Stalin's power and the main traffic junction for western Russia, through which passed nearly all of the Red Army's supplies. The loss of Moscow would have been a terrible blow to the Soviets and might even have unseated Stalin in an ugly internal power struggle.

While Leningrad was enduring the first days of an artillery and air siege, events were moving quickly in Ukraine. After building up a superiority of 2 to 1 in men and artillery and 1.5 to 1 in aircraft, on 30 July Hitler renewed the offensive along the Korosten–Berdichev–Letchev line. The first blow fell on the Kiev sector at the point where the 5th and 25th Armies touched. German troops had reached the outskirts of Kiev by 7 August but were driven back by a determined counterattack involving four rifle divisions of General A. A. Vlasov's 37th Army and two airborne corps used as infantry.

Meanwhile, Kleist's 1st Panzer Group managed to pierce the Soviet defences and outflank the 6th Army from the north in the area of Belaya Tserkov. At the same time the German 17th Army broke through the junction of the Soviet 12th and 18th Armies and began a two-pronged advance, one to the north to link up with Kleist and one south towards the Black Sea.

During the Soviet withdrawal, the 6th and 12th Armies were transferred to General Tyulenev's Southern Front and were about to escape the German pincers when Rundstedt switched Kleist's panzers from the Kiev sector to the Southern Front. This greatly speeded up the arms of the northern pincer and on 2 August Kleist severed the line of retreat of the 6th and 12th Armies east of Pervomaisk and linked up with the 17th Army advancing from Uman. The Soviet 6th and 12th Armies resisted until 12 August, when both army commanders were captured, along with many thousands of officers and men. Part of the 18th Army was also trapped. After the encirclement of the 6th and 12th Armies, German mobile forces pressed southward and by 19 August had reached the Black Sea port of Nikolaev, creating a threat to Odessa, which was evacuated by mid-October.

A far more serious threat was hanging over the Southwestern Front. On 8 August the 2nd Panzer Group began a new southward move against the Central Front in the area of Gomel. The Germans planned to encircle Soviet troops in the Kiev area by advancing from Gomel across the Desna to the area of Konotop–Sevsk in northern Ukraine. There they hoped to link up with Army Group South, fresh from its victory at Uman.

In mid-August Hitler's Directive 34 was followed by a supplementary directive that called on Army Group South to 'occupy the Donets area and the industrial area of Kharkov'. Despite the creation of the Bryansk Front under the Ukrainian General Eremenko, which counterattacked south of Smolensk in the last week of August, the Soviet Central Front disintegrated and the main weight of defending Kiev from the north and northeast fell on the already overstrained Southwestern Front.

After the battle for Kiev, Army Group Centre was instructed to remain on the defensive before Moscow while the 2nd Panzer Group switched northwards toward Bryansk and Kursk. Taking the panzer divisions' place was Walter von Reichenau's 6th Army and Carl-Heinrich von Stülpnagel's 17th Army. The strike formation of Army Group South, Paul Ludwig Ewald von Kleist's 1st Panzer Group, was sent south to strike towards Rostov-on-Don and the vital Caucasian oilfields. The 6th and 17th Armies spent three weeks regrouping and processing over half a million Red Army prisoners taken during the Battle of Kiev.

At the beginning of September the German 17th Army was told to 'gain ground in the direction of Poltava and Kharkov'. General von Kleist's panzers and the German 17th Army, after pushing the Red Army to the bend of the Dnieper, returned to the area of Kremenchug, where they began to force a crossing of the river 150 miles southeast of Kiev. In the first week of September the newly organised Soviet 40th Army, deployed to the right of the 5th Army, fell back east of Kharkov. Part of the 1st Panzer Group, along with the 17th Army, had completed the crossing of the Dnieper at Kremenchug on 12 September and drove back the Soviet 38th Army defending the river.

Three days later, on 17 September, the 1st and 2nd Panzer Groups met near Romny and the forces of the Southwestern Front were trapped. The Soviet 5th, 21st, 37th and 38th Armies, together with elements of the 40th and 26th Armies, were encircled. Control of these forces had collapsed as two days earlier Marshal Budenny had been relieved of his command for recommending the evacuation of Kiev, and the commander of the Southwestern Front, Colonel General M.P. Kirponos, and his chief of staff, General V.I. Tupikov, were killed by shellfire. The commander of the 5th Army, General M.I. Potapov, was captured, while the commander of the 24th Mechanised Corps, General V.I. Chistyakov, along with Generals D.S. Pisarevski, A.I. Zelentsov and K.Ya. Kulikov, was killed trying to escape the German trap. Estimates of the Red Army's losses vary but from a front of some 660,000 men about half were captured and fewer than 150,000 escaped east with their weapons.

At the end of September 1941 Marshal Timoshenko was appointed commander-in-chief of the battered Southwestern Strategic Sector. Nikita Khrushchev, who had previously served in Kiev under Budenny, was his chief political adviser or commissar and political member of the military council, and Major General A.P. Pokrovski was his chief of staff. Gathering what troops he could from the Kiev disaster, Timoshenko withdrew slowly to the line of the Donets River from Belgorod to Kharkov, while reserves were rushed to fill the gaps in his depleted order of battle.

A KV-2 'Dreadnought' captured during the Germans' swift advance. Those in the path of Army Group Centre were rapidly overrun. However, a tank such as this briefly held up Army Group North until its ammunition ran out.

This was the reality for most of the German units making up the three army groups that invaded the Soviet Union. The bulk of them were infantry divisions, which marched into Russia and Ukraine on foot. Army Group Centre was brought to a halt while operations were carried out against Leningrad in the north and Kiev to the south, and its panzers were redirected to help.

Despite the mechanisation of Hitler's Blitzkrieg, bicycle infantry made up a major part of the strength of German infantry divisions' reconnaissance units. These cyclists, along with men on motorcycles and horses, and in field and light armoured cars, often pushed far ahead of the rest of their division. In the second shot a motorcyclist has stopped to admire the imposing bulk of a KV-2 tank.

Getting across the Berezina, Dnieper, Desna and other major waterways required assault troops using inflatable rafts. It took nerves of steel, especially once the boat was exposed and under fire in the middle of the river.

When the Red Army demolished the bridges, German engineers swiftly replaced them. Nothing seemed to stop the Wehrmacht's Blitzkrieg.

German soldiers stand idly by while a Russian farmstead burns.

A German gunner prepares to soften up Soviet defensive positions. At every turn the Red Army's attempts to concentrate its forces and launch counterattacks were thwarted by artillery and air strikes.

The troops of Army Groups Centre and North could not believe the rapidity of their advance across the Soviet Union in the summer of 1941. Their victories inevitably meant that morale was high. These despatch riders in full field kit take time to pose for a snapshot.

German infantry entering a Russian or Ukrainian town. Snipers always posed a threat.

Soviet PoWs are marched past a Russian bear: the irony was lost on no one.

Mounted German troops pause to reflect on the fate of a Russian or Ukrainian soldier who lies by his overturned vehicle.

More Soviet prisoners. Following the battle for Minsk, the Red Army was defeated by Army Group Centre at Smolensk with the capture of 302,000 troops, 3,205 tanks, 3,120 guns and 1,098 aircraft.

The Red Air Force was either shot out of the sky or destroyed on the ground. The I-16 seen here was the first monoplane fighter to incorporate a retractable undercarriage and the first Soviet fighter to include armour around the cockpit.

Virtually all captured Soviet aircraft were unceremoniously scrapped by the Germans as the Luftwaffe had no use for them.

German personnel pause to admire their trophy: a large portrait of Stalin.

German wheeled and horse-drawn transport caught in the dust of the Russian summer. In the first shot an imposing church dominates the skyline.

A wounded Soviet prisoner is shown some compassion by his captors. The German in the middle appears to be from a Luftwaffe Field Division.

A panzertruppen confers with senior officers during a lull in the fighting.

A German poses with a dug in Maxim machine gun. It appears the gunners fled.

Another Maxim machine gun, the handle for towing the wheeled trolley is clearly visible.

After the victories of June-August 1941 medals are handed out by a rather portly German officer.

A German flak gun overlooks an enemy town.

Blitzkrieg fatalities on the Eastern Front, the Schutzmütze or black panzer beret (which incorporated a padded crash helmet) marks the three middle graves as panzertruppen. Although the Schutzmütze was discontinued in early 1941 and replaced by a field cap, it continued to be worn by crews of the Czech 38(t) panzer and armoured personnel carriers.

Chapter Four

First Battle for Kharkov – October 1941

By the end of July 1941 General Heinz Guderian was convinced that the key threat to Army Group Centre was not the Soviet 5th Army, which lay behind him, but the Red Army units gathering on his right flank north of the Russian town of Roslavl. In fact, these units were from the Soviet 28th Army under Lieutenant General Vladimir Kachalov, who had been tasked to relieve the Smolensk pocket with little more than three divisions. Guderian proposed to Bock that resources should be diverted south to take Roslavl. His attack opened on 2 August and two days later the town had been captured, along with 38,000 Soviet prisoners and 200 guns. The ease with which Guderian attained his victory should have warned him that this was not the main threat after all.

Eleven days had been wasted since the decision was taken to destroy the Soviet 5th Army. Even the destruction of the Soviet 16th Army and the 23rd Mechanised Corps on 5 August, along with elements of the 19th and 20th Armies, resulting in 300,000 prisoners, 3,200 tanks and 3,100 guns taken, could not compensate for this failure.

Budenny's request to withdraw his forces beyond the Dnieper was approved by Stavka (the Soviet high command) on 19 August. The Soviet 37th Army was ordered to remain in Kiev, but the withdrawn 5th Army and the new 40th Army (made up of remnants of other armies) were directed to form a line running southeast to protect Chernigov, Konotop and Kharkov. While this was a positive move, in reality Budenny's forces were already expended and he had no reserves left for his Southwestern Front. Everything depended on Yeremenko's Western Front to defend Moscow.

Once the Battle of Moscow was under way, Hitler had to safeguard his flanks. On 6 October Reichenau's 6th Army moved in the direction of Belgorod and Kharkov, driving through Sumy and Okhtyrka. At the same time Stülpnagel's 17th Army moved to protect the lengthening flank of the 1st Panzer Army (formerly the 1st

Panzer Group). This was achieved by launching an offensive from Poltava towards Lozova and Izyum.

Hitler allocated units from the 17th Army to assist the 6th Army with the capture of Kharkov. The result of this was to greatly weaken the 17th Army's attempts to screen the 1st Panzer Army's flank and this contributed to the German defeat at the Battle of Rostov. The task of capturing Kharkov was assigned to General Erwin Vierow's 55th Corps, comprising General Josef Brauner von Haydringen's 101st Light Division and General Anton Dostler's 57th Infantry Division. The latter was supported by two batteries from Sturmgeschütz Battalion 197, commanded by Captain Kurt von Barisani.

General von Haydringen's men had fought their way to within 4 miles of the city by 21 October. By now the *Rasputitsa* or muddy season had begun to close in with the autumn and it wasn't until the middle of the month that the night frosts hardened up the roads. The gathering snow and the fall in temperatures hit the Germans hard as they had not been issued with winter clothing.

Haydringen's 228th Light Regiment acted as spearhead, with the 1st and 3rd Battalions at the front and the 2nd Battalion in reserve. On 22 October the regiment was instructed to probe the Red Army's forward defences, held by the 216th Rifle Division. This comprised a Soviet infantry battalion, supported by tanks that launched an attack at noon that day.

On 23 October Haydringen's 3rd Battalion was strengthened by two guns from the 85th Artillery Regiment, a single 88mm anti-aircraft gun and a company of engineers. The 2nd Battalion was similarly reinforced but lacked an anti-aircraft gun. This time the 1st Battalion was assigned the role of regimental reserve. In addition, the 1st Battalion from the 229th Light Regiment was to act as flank guard while the 228th attacked, along with the German 57th Infantry Regiment.

The attack on Kharkov was set for noon but the artillery was not ready so the attack had to be postponed until 3pm. Likewise there were problems moving the anti-tank company forward as it fell foul of the mud. When it did arrive, it was instructed to allot a 37mm gun platoon to each of the front-line battalions.

As the evacuation of the city had already been completed, the Red Army was not obliged to conduct any major defensive operations. The escape of the city's factories, especially the T-34 plant, was to cost the Germans dearly in the coming years. Resistance by the Soviet 216th Division was feeble and did little to hamper the German advance. By 24 October 1941 Kharkov was firmly in the hands of Dostler's 57th Infantry Division.

Administration of the city was given to 55th Corps, with the 57th Division acting as the occupation force. But the Red Army had left a nasty surprise for the Germans. On 14 November a series of bombs on time fuses exploded in a number of buildings, killing General Georg Braun and his staff from the 68th Infantry Division. Reprisals were swift; some 200 civilians were arrested, many of them Jews, who were hanged from the balconies of the city's major buildings. A month later the SS of Einsatzgruppe C herded 20,000 Jews into a hut settlement near the Kharkov Tractor Factory, where they were methodically exterminated. To add to the city's woes, the German garrison confiscated much of the available food, causing shortages for the civilian population. By January 1942 the population had been reduced to 300,000 and many people faced starvation.

Meanwhile, the defence of Moscow had become a priority for the Red Army. Stavka's plan called for an offensive by all three fronts in the Moscow area: Konev's Kalinin Front to the north of the Sea of Moscow, Zhukov's Western Front on either side of the capital and Timoshenko's Southwestern Front on Zhukov's left flank. Zhukov would provide the main effort; on his right the fresh 1st Shock and 20th Armies were to open the attack, supported by the 30th and 16th Armies on the flanks. They were to link up with Konev's 29th and 31st Armies. The intention was that Zhukov's front would tie down German forces opposite Moscow, while the 10th and 50th Armies on the southern wing, along with Timoshenko's forces, attacked Guderian's Panzer Group.

Lelyushenko's 30th Army at Dmitrov, to the north of Moscow, made the deepest penetration into German lines on the first day, advancing to the Moscow–Leningrad Highway and threatening the junction between the German 4th Army and the 4th Panzer Group. After three days it had reached Klin and, with the 1st Shock Army on the left flank, seemed poised to achieve a successful encirclement. Rokossovsky's 16th Army and Vlasov's 20th Army made equally pleasing progress, taking Istra west of Moscow by the 13th.

The Soviet 13th and 40th Armies belonging to Timoshenko's mauled Southwestern Front pierced the southern face of the 3rd Panzer Group salient, which had been created in November. By 9 December Timoshenko was threatening the Germans' main supply route, the Orel–Tula railway. In the meantime the 50th and 10th Armies struck the northern edge of the salient, driving a wedge between Guderian and Kluge. Once the Soviet 33rd and 43rd Armies had joined the offensive on 18 December, the German 4th Army was increasingly pushed back westward.

To the north Konev's Kalinin Front drove the German 9th Army from Kalinin and thrust southwestwards along the Upper Volga towards Rzhev. In the far south Rundstedt was ejected from Rostov-on-Don on 28 November, having occupied it only five days previously. Hitler, incensed that his generals had not taken Moscow, sacked Field Marshal von Brauchitsch, CinC Army, Bock, Leeb and Guderian, while Rundstedt was transferred west. Thirty-five corps or divisional commanders were also removed. The loss of Rostov was the first significant German withdrawal of the war.

Lance Corporal Siegfried Lämmel was shot in the head on 10 August 1941 during the fighting in the Soviet Union. Perhaps his shaken-looking comrades from a Luftwaffe field unit took this photograph to send home to his family. His simple grave would soon be joined by tens of thousands of others.

German troops file past an abandoned B-5 fast tank. This design went into production in Kharkov in the mid-1930s. It was followed by the improved BT-7, identifiable by its conical (rather than cylindrical) turret. Both were superseded by the T-34.

German heavy field guns prepare to bombard Soviet defences.

German infantry moving through Russia. The 6th Army, with the assistance of units from the 17th Army, was instructed to take Kharkov. This was a decision that cost Hitler the Battle of Rostov.

Knocked-out Soviet T-26 tanks. The main priority for the 38th Army was to conduct an orderly withdrawal in the face of the German advance, rather than defend Kharkov. Once the city's military factories had been safely evacuated, the Red Army largely abandoned it.

A German Army Opel Blitz truck hastens through a war-torn Soviet town. The extensive damage indicates that it had been visited by the Luftwaffe.

A column of lorries waiting in a burnt-out street – perhaps another target of Luftwaffe bombing.

The presence of German occupation forces did not stop the locals going about their day-to-day business.

German lorries gathered beneath an impressive Russian Orthodox church.

This GAZ-AAA cargo truck was caught in the open. The driver lies dead at the roadside. All Soviet movements were at the mercy of the Luftwaffe. The GAZ factory was based in Gorky and drew on American Ford designs.

These three Red Army ZPU anti-aircraft trucks were caught either by German artillery or by air attack. This rudimentary self-propelled anti-aircraft gun provided no protection for the crew.

Bemused-looking Ukrainian youths pose for the camera.

A German soldier trying to photograph the destruction wrought by fleeing Soviet troops. Such blazes were left to burn themselves out for fear of snipers.

German infantry and panzertruppen pause to bury their dead.

Withdrawing Red Army units set fire to anything that might be of use to the advancing German Army. Equally, this could have been the handiwork of the Luftwaffe's Stuka dive-bombers.

A German column passing a KV-1 heavy tank. It appears its crew may have attempted to entrench it to afford it better protection. If that's the case, it is clearly facing the wrong way. The only other explanation is that it was withdrawing and become stuck in a bomb crater.

A German assault gun and half-track supporting infantry battling Soviet defenders on the streets of Kharkov.

More German armoured vehicles on the streets of Kharkov. By 24 October 1941 the city was firmly in the hands of the 57th Infantry Division. The Soviet 38th Army had given up the fight and withdrawn to lick its wounds.

Germans pose in the remains of a wrecked Su-2 short-range bomber. This aircraft was initially built in Kharkov until the factory was evacuated to Molotov with enough components to keep production going until the end of April 1942. At this stage of the fighting the Soviet Air Force was able to offer little support to the beleaguered Red Army, having been destroyed on the ground and in the sky.

Occupation forces move in. The large number of staff vehicles indicate that this is a HQ unit looking for a suitable billet.

A photo for back home: two men in a motorbike and sidecar sightsee in Kharkov's imposing Dzerzhinsky Square.

A Panzer Mk III keeps the peace in Dzerzhinsky Square.

The Red Army booby-trapped Kharkov with a series of bombs which exploded on 14 November 1941, killing the commander of the German 68th Infantry Division and his staff. In reprisal, 200 civilians were hanged from prominent balconies as a warning to the rest of the population.

A quarry acts as a holding pen for thousands of Soviet prisoners. Along with the civilians in the occupied zones, they faced a miserable winter as food supplies became scarce.

A German cargo truck getting a tow through the mud and snow of the dreaded Russian *rasputitsa* or quagmire season. The WH prefix on the number plate stands for Wehrmacht (or armed forces) and Heer (or army). The weather did not bring an end to the fighting but greatly hampered it.

Judging by their fresh and uniform appearance, these German infantrymen are newly arrived on the front line.

Chapter Five

Second Battle for Kharkov – May 1942

The second battle for Kharkov was to be a vastly bigger and more costly affair than the first. By early 1942 Stalin's winter counteroffensive, which halted Hitler at the very gates of Moscow, had run out of steam and both sides paused to regroup. Stalin convinced himself that the German Army was now spent and could not cope with Mother Russia's bitter winter. He was confident that he could roll the Nazis back, but he was grossly overestimating the capabilities of the exhausted and much-depleted Red Army.

Stalin, much encouraged by the Red Army's last-ditch efforts in stopping the Wehrmacht, was determined to launch another counteroffensive to capitalise on the situation. On 5 January 1942 he told his gathered generals:

> The Germans are in disarray as a result of their defeat before Moscow. They've prepared badly for the winter. This is the most favourable moment to go over to a general offensive. The Germans hope to hold our offensive until the spring, so that they can resume active operations when they have built up their strength.
>
> Our task is therefore to give the Germans no time to draw breath, to drive them to the west, and to force them to use up all their reserves before spring comes because by then we will have new reserves and the German reserves will have run out.

This was sound military thinking, but it did not take into account either the resilience of the Wehrmacht or the true offensive capabilities of the Red Army. Stalin envisaged that the main effort would be against Army Group Centre, with the aim of trapping it west of Vyazma; meanwhile the Leningrad and Volkhov Fronts were to crush Army Group North and save Leningrad. It would be Timoshenko's job to deal with Army Group South, liberating Kharkov, the Donbas and Sevastopol in the Crimea. The attack towards Kharkov was to be two-pronged, from Volchansk to the northeast of the city and from Barvenkovo to the south.

On 5 April 1942 Hitler issued Directive 41, which struck an equally confident note: 'The winter battle in Russia is nearing its end. Thanks to the unequalled courage and self-sacrificing devotion on the Eastern Front, German arms have achieved a great defensive success.' He then laid out his plans for the coming summer, which gave the Wehrmacht the task of ejecting the Red Army from the Don region, the Donbas industrial region, the Caucasian oilfields and the Caucasus passes. He hoped that the latter operations would encourage neutral Turkey to finally side with the Axis. Outlining his *General Plan*, Hitler stated:

> In pursuit of the original plan for the Eastern campaign, the armies of the Central sector [Army Group Centre] will stand fast, those in the *North* [Army Group North] will capture Leningrad and link up with the Finns, while those on the *southern flank* [Army Group South] will break through into the Caucasus. In view of the conditions prevailing at the end of winter, the availability of troops and resources, and transport problems, these aims can be achieved only one at a time.
>
> First, therefore, all available forces will be concentrated on the *main operations in the southern sector*, with the aim of destroying the enemy before the Don, in order to secure the Caucasian oilfields and the passes through the Caucasus mountains themselves.

In early 1942 the Germans began to conduct a deception plan, codenamed Kremlin, which was designed to convince Stalin that the German summer offensive would be directed towards finally capturing Moscow. 'Information' was leaked to foreign newspapers, while Army Group Centre conducted poorly concealed preparations which seemed to indicate that Hitler would again attack the Soviet capital in force.

In the meantime, during the spring of 1942 the Germans began preparing for their real summer offensive, a massive southern assault known as Operation Blue. Their first moves were to secure their flanks. Way to the south, this meant driving the Red Army completely from the Crimea and capturing Sevastopol. This would both protect the right flank of Field Marshal Fedor von Bock's Army Group South and enable General Erich von Manstein's 11th Army to cross the Straits of Kerch in support of the 1st Panzer Army and the 17th Army's offensive along the eastern coast of the Black Sea once they were across the lower Don and Donets.

Manstein moved to eliminate the Red Army from the Kerch peninsula on 8 May 1942 with Operation Bustard Trap. He diverted all his forces except for his 54th Corps and the Romanian Army, which remained before Sevastopol. In total, six German and three Romanian divisions were thrown at the Soviet 44th, 47th and 51st Armies. The Germans, with Luftwaffe support, sliced through the thin Soviet defences.

By the evening, Manstein's 30th Corps had pierced the Soviet 44th Army's front and eleven Soviet divisions were driven into the Sea of Azov on 11 May. The rest of Manstein's forces reached Kerch five days later. The Soviets could not hold on in the Crimea and evacuated, and in the chaos that followed they lost 170,000 prisoners, 260 tanks, 1,140 guns and 300 aircraft. Manstein's forces in contrast suffered 7,500 casualties. He could now devote all his attention to reducing the last remaining Soviet stronghold in the Crimea: Sevastopol. This was defended by about 100,000 men of Lieutenant General I.E. Petrov's Independent Coastal Command.

In Ukraine, while Timoshenko and his Southwestern Front were preparing to liberate Kharkov, Bock's Army Group South was planning to destroy the Barvenkovo–Lozovaya bridgehead that stretched west from Izyum beyond the Donets south of Kharkov. General Friedrich Paulus deployed his forces between Belgorod and Balakleya, north and south of Kharkov respectively, while Kleist further to the south was at Pavlograd, west of the Soviet bridgehead. Their intention was to cut off and destroy the Soviet salient, straighten the German line along the Donets and then launch their main offensive. Ironically, Timoshenko obliged Bock by putting more Soviet troops into the noose.

This salient had been created by a Soviet offensive launched on 18 January against Army Group South. The intention was for the Soviet 6th, 57th and 9th Armies of the Southwestern Front, as well as the South Front, to drive west over the Donets between Balakleya in the north and Artemovsk in the south, before swinging south to the Sea of Azov at Melitopol, trapping German forces in the area. However, in the event the South Front never got beyond its start point and the Southwestern Front ground to a halt on 31 January, having created a considerable salient containing two armies.

Nikita Khrushchev, head of the communist party in Ukraine and Stalin's regional enforcer (his official title was Military Commissar of the Southwestern Direction), recalled, 'Perhaps my most perilous hour was during the disastrous counteroffensive towards Kharkov in 1942. We had broken through the enemy's front line of defence easily – too easily. We realised that there were no forces massed against us. We seemed to have a clear road ahead, deep into enemy territory. This was unsettling. It meant we had stumbled into a trap.'

Disastrously, two-thirds of the Soviet armour, along with General Kharitonov's 9th Army and General Gorodnyanski's 6th Army, moved into the salient ready to liberate Krasnograd southwest of Kharkov. This was to be followed by a push on Kharkov and Poltava way to the west. Their attack was to be supported by the Soviet 28th and 38th Armies northeast of Kharkov in the Volchansk bridgehead.

If Bock had struck first, he would have had to contend with nearly 600 Soviet tanks, but as it turned out Timoshenko pipped him to the post by attacking a week earlier on 12 May. The Soviet forces launched from Volchansk made little impression against Paulus' fourteen divisions, but in the south Romanian forces could not prevent the fall of Krasnograd and it seemed Kharkov was within Timoshenko's grasp. The Soviet 9th Army rolled on to Karlovka, west of Kharkov. Worryingly, though, the Red Army was unable to widen the breach south of Izyum and Barvenkovo, which meant the pocket got bigger but the breach did not.

If the Soviet 6th and 9th Armies had both struck towards Merefa, just south of Kharkov, things might have gone differently, but as Kharitonov's 9th Army headed west on the 17th warning signs began to appear. This was the Soviets' first attempt at an armoured offensive on this scale but it had clearly not brought the Germans' main combat strength to battle: this was now identified as lying on their southern flank. It was imperative for the Soviets to shift to a defensive posture and move their armour, anti-tank guns and artillery to protect their exposed left flank. Realising the danger, Timoshenko and Khrushchev (serving as the front's commissar) called a halt to the Soviet advance with a view to helping the 9th Army, only for their command to be overridden by Stalin. Despite Khrushchev's efforts to get Stalin to stop the offensive, his orders were to press on.

On the 18th the Germans counterattacked. Eleven divisions from Kleist's Army Group struck from Slavyansk–Kramatorsk, hitting the 9th and 57th Armies, and within two days had broken out on the left wing of the Southwestern Front. Kleist was assaulting the left flank of the salient northwards towards Izyum in an attempt to cut off the 57th and 9th Armies, as well as the 6th Army and Group Bobrin (the last two had been halted in the preceding days trying to push westward towards Krasnograd on the key railway line southwest of Kharkov). Izyum was taken on the 18th and the Soviets fell back in a state of chaos as the Germans sped on to reach the Oskol river.

'Catastrophe struck a few days later,' says Khrushchev, 'exactly as we expected. There was nothing we could do to avert it. Many generals, colonels, junior officers and troops perished. The staff of the 57th Army was wiped out completely. Almost nobody managed to escape. The army had advanced deep into enemy territory, and when our men were encircled, they didn't even have enough fuel to escape. It was too far to return on foot. Many were killed, but most taken prisoner. General Gurov somehow managed to escape in a tank.'

With the noose tightening around the Soviet forces, Timoshenko dispatched his deputy, General Kostenko, to try to save the 6th and 9th Armies. When General Friedrich Paulus' panzers arrived at Balakleya on 23 May, linking up with those of Kleist, the trap snapped shut. By the 26th the survivors were squeezed into an area of about 15 square kilometres. The main areas of resistance were quickly broken up into a series of ever-shrinking pockets that were swiftly overwhelmed. Less than a quarter of the two Soviet armies got away, and all their heavy equipment was left littering the west bank of the Donets.

Officially, the Soviets acknowledged 5,000 killed (including General Kuzma Podlas, the commander of the 57th Army), 70,000 missing and 300 tanks lost. The Germans claimed to have captured 240,000 men, a figure that Khrushchev confirmed to Stalin when he reported to Moscow shortly after. This implied that the bulk of the Soviet troops surrendered. The Germans also claimed to have taken or destroyed 1,200 tanks. In fact, Timoshenko only had 845 tanks in total, but the German figure may include all armoured fighting vehicles. It is doubtful whether any Soviet armour escaped the southern pocket, although the 28th Army may have saved a few tanks in the north.

In the face of such an unmitigated disaster, Timoshenko sought to gather his remaining troops by appealing to their stomachs. When Khrushchev returned from a tense meeting with Stalin in Moscow, he observed, 'Marshal Timoshenko told me that the army had been so utterly routed by the enemy that the only way to rally the troops was to set up mobile kitchens and hope the soldiers would return when they got hungry. He was drawing on his Civil War experience here. We set up field kitchens and slowly but surely reorganised our defences.'

The cost of the failed Kharkov offensive for the Red Army was considerable. During 1942 the tank ratio had stood at five to one in their favour, but it was now ten to one against them, which did not bode well in light of the coming German summer offensive. Operation Fridericus II, intended to clear the Kupyansk area and secure a bridgehead over the Oskol, followed on 22–26 June. Moving from southeast of Kharkov, the Soviets were again driven back, losing 40,000 more prisoners and sealing the destruction of the Southwestern Front.

Inevitably, someone had to take the blame for the failed Kharkov offensive and initially Khrushchev feared he was going to face a firing squad when he flew to Moscow. Certainly Stalin accused Khrushchev of acting independently of Timoshenko in halting the offensive and going over to the defensive. Khrushchev denied this, saying he had Timoshenko's agreement. Both men knew it was the only logical course of action.

To be fair, despite the wrangling with Stalin, the Red Army was not given time to react, because by the time the danger was appreciated, the Germans had launched their counteroffensive and their deadly encirclement was rapidly under way. Rather unfairly, as a consequence of the Kharkov disaster Timoshenko was demoted from Deputy People's Commissar of Defence and CinC Southwestern Strategic Sector. Zhukov in contrast took over as Deputy Supreme Commander under Stalin, his star in the ascendancy.

Saboteurs in Kharkov and other Soviet cities faced summary execution in a very public place. Designed to cow the civilian population, such acts often had the reverse effect and drove them to join the partisans, seeking vengeance.

German transport struggling in the mud of the spring thaw. The first vehicle appears to be an Opel Blitz and the second a Mercedes-Benz. Such weather greatly helped Soviet defensive operations.

A disabled Soviet T-26 tank. This example has the sloped turret, while the one in the background is fitted with the earlier cylindrical version. On 18 January 1942 three Soviet armies struck German positions near Izyum along the Northern Donets river south of Kharkov, taking the rail junctions at Lozovaya and Barvenkovo. By early May the Soviet salient contained at least half a dozen Soviet tank brigades, many of which were still equipped with the inadequate T-26 and BT-7 tank designs.

A Soviet BT tank amidst the corn. After the Red Army attack opened on 12 May 1942, Timoshenko's tanks were soon rolling towards Krasnograd and Pavlograd. The former was captured but the Soviets were held east of the latter. The lack of German resistance soon began to ring alarm bells with Soviet commanders.

A German gunner manning an MG 34 – the standard support weapon of the Wehrmacht.

German troops examining an abandoned BT tank. Its very narrow tracks were not well suited to the muddy conditions. Northeast of Kharkov Soviet forces made very little headway from the Volchansk bridgehead and provided no support for the southern pincer.

A T-26 and a smashed statue of Lenin now in German hands.

Dead Red Army soldiers lie strewn in a ditch. The initial lightness of the German resistance in the spring of 1942 led Timoshenko and Khrushchev to believe they were walking into a trap and they wanted to call a halt to their Izyum offensive.

On 18 May 1942 the Germans counterattacked the Barvenkovo bridgehead, rapidly revealing how exposed the Red Army's position was west of the Donets. These German infantry are mopping up after catching Soviet infantry in the open.

This Maxim gunner was caught in the open by a German counterattack. German troops and vehicles are just visible beyond the railway embankment in the background.

A Soviet casualty among the trees. The Wehrmacht's second victory at Kharkov cost it around 20,000 killed, wounded, missing or captured.

A local peasant collects the dead for burial.

These Soviet prisoners are wearing the *pilotka* or side cap that was authorised for all ranks in 1935.

Stalin insisted that the Southwestern Front hold the Barvenkovo bridgehead and maintain its offensive. As a result, the trapped Army Group Kostenko, including the Soviet 6th and 57th Armies, was destroyed, the men either killed or captured. These prisoners are mostly wearing the *budenovka* cloth helmet or *ushanka* with fur flaps.

Most of these Red Army prisoners are wearing cloth side caps or woollen caps, but the man in the middle has retained his M1940 helmet. Many troops were also still wearing the more distinctive M1936 helmet, which from a distance resembled the German M35/40 helmets.

A prisoner of war from one of the Soviet Central Asian republics. Clearly his convoy failed to escape the grasp of the German Army. Manpower shortages forced the Red Army to recruit from the Soviet Muslim ethnic minorities in the Caucasus, Central Asia and the Far East, despite the language assimilation problems that this presented.

A female Red Army commissar is led away for interrogation. Political commissars (*komissars* or *Politruks*) had the same uniforms as their army counterparts, but were not entitled to gold edging on their collar patches or sleeve chevrons. A further distinction was a red cloth five-pointed star on the lower left sleeve. Her *furashka* peaked cap automatically marked her out as an authority figure and therefore of interest to her captors.

Smiles all round: reward for a job well done.

During the summer of 1942 the Soviets lost another 40,000 men taken prisoner southeast of Kharkov.

A German field kitchen negotiates the Russian landscape.

Rest and recreation after the victory: eager German troops queue for a field cinema.

With the Red Army defeated around Kharkov, Ukrainian partisans were rounded up and executed.

Chapter Six

Third Battle for Kharkov – February 1943

By early 1943 one of Stalin's priorities was another attempt to liberate Ukraine's second city. On 12 January 1943 a general Soviet offensive began with the intention of pushing Field Marshal Maximilian Freiherr von Weichs' Army Group A and Field Marshal Erich von Manstein's Army Group Don away from the Don and into Ukraine. The offensive opened between Orel in the north and Rostov in the south and employed Lieutenant General M.A. Reiter's Bryansk Front, Colonel General F.I. Golikov's Voronezh Front, General N.F. Vatutin's Southwestern Front and General A.I. Eremenko's South Front. It was resisted by the German 2nd, Hungarian 2nd, Italian 8th and Romanian 3rd Armies and the German 4th Panzer Army.

By the end of January Army Group A's 17th Army was isolated in the Kuban. The battered Army Group B was placed into reserve and its formations given to Army Groups Centre and South. Fortunately for the Germans, the Red Army now began to lose some of its initial momentum. Pressing forward to the Oskol, Donets and Don rivers, as well as thrusting to the southwest to Kharkov, the Soviets also opted to punch west towards Kursk in order to exploit the 200-mile gap torn between Field Marshal von Kluge's Army Group Centre and Manstein's Army Group Don (soon renamed South).

On 1 February 1943 Stalin launched Operation Star, with the 13th and 38th Armies of the Voronezh Front attacking towards Kursk and the 60th, 40th and 3rd Tank Armies striking for Kharkov. In the meantime the Southwestern Front's 6th Army and the 1st Guards Army swung to the southwest to take Mariupol on the Sea of Azov, cutting Army Group Don's communications with Army Group A in the Caucasus.

Spearheading Star was Lieutenant General P.S. Rybalko's 3rd Tank Army on the Voronezh Front's southern flank. By 5 February (three days after the last pocket of German resistance in Stalingrad surrendered) he had reached the Donets east of Kharkov. The Voronezh Front liberated Volchansk, Belgorod, Oboyan and Kursk and by 11 February 1943 had successfully reached the outskirts of Kharkov. Meanwhile the Southwestern Front was soon deep in the rear of Army Group Don. The Soviets had every prospect of trapping the 1st Panzer Army, the 4th Panzer Army and Army Group Hollidt against the Sea of Azov. Only after the personal intervention of Kluge and Manstein did Hitler agree to a withdrawal to the River Mius.

At Kharkov the newly arrived I SS Panzer Corps under General Paul Hausser stood in the Soviets' way but was pushed back. Fearing that Kharkov could become another Stalingrad, Hausser disobeyed Hitler's orders to stand firm and withdrew from the city on 15 February. Manstein was concerned that Army Detachment Lanz was expected both to hold Kharkov and to strike towards Losovaya to relieve the pressure on Army Group South's left flank. It was only in a position to conduct one of the two tasks and Manstein wanted to avoid another Stalingrad at all costs. His proposal was to abandon Kharkov, strike south to defeat the Red Army and then reoccupy the city. Hitler, though, did not want to relinquish his hold on the Soviet Union's fourth largest city. In the event, Hausser's withdrawal to avoid being surrounded enabled Manstein to withdraw his forces as well.

To compound Manstein's problems, Hitler flew into the factory town of Zaporozhye southwest of Kharkov to be briefed on the situation. Alarmingly, the Field Marshal was unable to guarantee Hitler's safety as the town was only garrisoned by a defence company and a few anti-aircraft units. When they met on 17 February Hitler refused to discuss Manstein's plans and would not accept that the Red Army posed a very dangerous threat to the junction between the 1st Panzer Army and Army Detachment Lanz.

Manstein assumed this was because Hitler was keen to see the SS Panzer Corps rumble back into Kharkov, but the reality was that the threat to the Dnieper crossings had to be dealt with first. Also, it was now a race against time as the impending thaw would soon put a halt to operations between the Dnieper and Donets rivers.

The mud actually came to Manstein's rescue because the 3rd SS Panzer Division became bogged down between Kiev and Poltava. If the 1st and 2nd SS Panzer Divisions were not comfortable holding the city on their own, they were unlikely to retake it without the assistance of their sister division. In the light of this, Hitler acquiesced to Manstein's plans but refused to countenance shortening the 470-mile front held by Army Group South's battered thirty divisions. Despite Manstein's intelligence, Hitler also refused to acknowledge the Red Army's gathering strength in manpower and tanks. As Manstein observed diplomatically, 'We lived, it seemed, in two entirely different worlds.' Perhaps more importantly he noted, 'I had the impression that Hitler's visit to my headquarters had helped to bring home to him the danger of encirclement which immediately threatened the southern wing of the Eastern Front.'

In the meantime the main Soviet threat was a salient thrusting towards Dnepropetrovsk, containing the 1st Guards and 6th Armies as well as Group Popov. While the Germans held the Red Army west of Kharkov, Manstein orchestrated a counterattack on 19 February using the II SS Panzer Corps striking south from Krasnograd, southwest of Kharkov, towards Pavlograd. Three days later Hoth's 4th Panzer Army linked up with the SS at Pavlograd.

On the southern side of the salient the 1st Panzer Army's 40th Panzer Corps joined the attack defeating Group Popov near Krasnoarmeysk. The Soviets interpreted these operations as a means of covering the 1st Panzer Army's and Army Group Hollidt's withdrawal from the Mius to the Dnieper. In response, the Southwestern Front was instructed to hold the Germans on the Mius. However, Manstein's success at Pavlograd had enabled his forces to push forwards 150 miles, thereby threatening recently liberated Kharkov. Indeed, Manstein had unhinged the junction of the Soviet Southwestern and Voronezh Fronts. In the fighting the Soviet advances were brought to a standstill, having lost 23,000 men dead and 9,000 captured, along with 615 tanks and 354 artillery pieces.

Having gained victory between the Donets and Dnieper, the Germans were ready to tackle those Red Army units in the vicinity of Kharkov. Now Manstein was very clear on what was to happen: 'Our object was not the possession of Kharkov but the defeat – and if possible the destruction – of the enemy units located there.' This principally meant crushing the Soviet 3rd Tank Army using the 4th Panzer Army and the SS Panzer Corps.

General Rybalko's 3rd Tank Army swung south to take on the I SS Panzer Corps on 24 February. The SS withdrew to lure the Soviets into a trap, which resulted in the Red Army losing another 9,000 men killed, 61 tanks, 60 motor vehicles and 225 guns. Rybalko's defeat left newly liberated Kharkov open to the Germans once more. His 3rd Tank Army now had to fight its way out of the Kharkov area and Stalin agreed to a withdrawal to the Donets from 40 miles away.

'In the end it was possible to bring the SS Panzer Corps round to the east. The city fell without difficulty, and we succeeded in cutting off the retreat of considerable numbers of the enemy across the Donets,' recorded Manstein in his usual no-nonsense manner.

Following the Soviet victory at Stalingrad, in early February 1943 Stavka planned an offensive to capitalise on the successes of the Bryansk and Voronezh Fronts along the Voronezh–Kursk axis and support the Southwestern Front's push through the Donbas to the Dnieper and the Sea of Azov. This was scheduled to begin on 12 February, when the Western Front's 16th Army and the Bryansk Front's 13th and 48th Armies were to surround the Germans' Orel salient. The two fronts, supported by the Central Front, were to clear the Bryansk region and gain bridgeheads over the Desna between the 17th and 25th. Afterwards the Kalinin and Western Fronts were to take Smolensk and help destroy Army Group Centre in the Rzhev–Viazma salient.

General K.K. Rokossovsky's Don Front (formerly the Stalingrad Front) attempted a left hook behind the Orel salient, launched from the Soviet salient around Kursk; this offensive was halted by the German 2nd Army at Sevsk. In the Donbas Manstein threw back the Southwestern Front, and the Western Front failed in the Zhizdra area.

Rokossovksy's offensive was delayed to 25 February. His Don Front (renamed the Central Front) was spearheaded by the 2nd Tank Army and 70th Army from Stavka reserve, together with the 65th and 21st Armies redeployed from Stalingrad. Within two weeks the 2nd Tank Army had gained Sevsk, while a Cavalry-Rifle Group from the 2nd Guards Cavalry Corps reached Trubchevsk and Novgorod-Seversky. However, south of Orel the progress of the 65th and 70th Armies was slow and on the left flank the 38th and 60th Armies were tied up trying to turn the German 2nd Army's left flank.

Rokossovsky was denied victory by bad weather, the delayed arrival of the 21st Army from Stalingrad (which was subsequently diverted to Oboyan to counter Manstein's move on Belgorod), and by Manstein's counterstroke that smashed the Voronezh Front south of Kharkov. The fighting continued until 23 March, but Rokossovsky's troops gave up Sevsk to take up positions that would become the northern and central face of the Kursk salient.

Field Marshal von Manstein was then able to launch the second phase of his powerful counteroffensive on 6 March, and by 14 March he was back in control of Kharkov. The Germans claimed to have killed another 50,000 Soviets and captured 19,594, as well as destroying 1,140 tanks and 3,000 guns. In just over two months the SS Panzer Corps had sustained over 11,000 casualties; the 1st SS Panzer Division lost 4,500 of these during the recapture of Kharkov.

Manstein recorded with some satisfaction his remarkable victory at Kharkov, but also noted a lost opportunity against the Soviets' Kursk salient:

> On 14 March Kharkov fell to the SS Panzer Corps. At the same time on the northern wing Army Detachment Kempf, the 'Gross-Deutschland' Division, moved swiftly to Belgorod. The enemy once again threw in strong armoured forces to oppose it, but these were wiped out at Gaivoron.
>
> The capture of Kharkov and Belgorod marked the conclusion of Army Group's second counterblow, as the increasing muddiness of the ground did not permit any further operations. As a matter of fact the Army Group would have liked to wind up by clearing out, with the help of Central Army Group,

the enemy salient extending some distance westwards of Kursk in order to shorten the German front. The scheme had to be abandoned, however, as Central Army Group declared itself unable to co-operate. As a result the salient continued to constitute a troublesome dent in our front . . .

Alarmed by the situation in the south, Stalin summoned Zhukov, his deputy supreme commander, to Moscow on the 14th. Zhukov found himself sent to the Voronezh Front, where his prognosis was dire: 'All available forces from the Stavka's reserves must be deployed here, otherwise the Germans will capture Belgorod and continue their offensive on the Kursk sector.'

Stalin had already decided to dispatch the 1st Tank, 21st and 64th Armies to the Belgorod area, but they could not be in place quickly enough to save the city, which fell to Manstein on the 18th. None the less, the Soviet 21st and 64th Armies were able to move into blocking positions northeast of Belgorod and this thwarted Manstein's attempt on Kursk.

Once the three Soviet divisions (52nd Guards, 67th Guards Rifle and 375th Rifle) from the 21st Army had taken up defensive positions, the Germans were unable to dislodge them. The 1st Tank Army deployed south of Oboyan and the 64th Army along the Seversky Donets. By 26 March Zhukov had managed to stabilise the line and the spring thaw brought the mobile warfare to a halt. The Germans in turn dug in.

General von Mellenthin was fulsome in his praise for Manstein's achievements: 'Having regard to the problems which faced Manstein between December 1942 and February 1943, it may be questioned whether any achievement of generalship in World War II can approach the successful extrication of the Caucasus armies, and the subsequent riposte to Kharkov.'

In a stroke of genius Manstein had defeated Stalin's Operation Star. He had saved Army Group South and put the Germans back on the Mius/Donets line. While impressive, such a victory could not offset the disaster at Stalingrad. Although checked by the II SS Panzer Corps, the Red Army threatened the whole region from Kharkov via Belgorod to Kursk. The latter would ultimately be Hitler's undoing on the Eastern Front.

After the dismal failure of the Red Army to liberate Kharkov in the spring of 1942, the battered city languished under German rule throughout the summer and autumn. The remaining population lived as best they could amongst the ruins.

While the German occupation forces settled down for the winter, Stalin began to plan an offensive to drive the Wehrmacht away from the Don and into the Ukraine.

A German flak gun position. Unbeknown to the German garrison at Kharkov, on 1 February 1943 Operation Star launched three armies with a view to liberating the city.

A series of shots showing German MG34 gunners. In the first two, gunners stand on guard wrapped against the bitter Russian winter. In the first photo the spent shell cases show that the weapon has recently been fired; in the third, the weapon is mounted on a raised tripod for anti-aircraft use.

Once the Soviet 3rd Tank Army had reached the Donets to the east of Kharkov, Field Marshal von Manstein, commanding Army Group South, knew Army Detachment Lanz could not hold the city and help him at the same time. He wanted to evacuate Kharkov but Hitler would have none of it. However, when General Paul Hausser's I SS Panzer Corps abandoned the city, Hitler acquiesced to the withdrawal of Army Detachment Lanz.

For the third time the people of Kharkov found their city a battleground for the opposing armies.

German solders guard the tramlines from saboteurs.

Luftwaffe groundcrew prepare to move a two-seater Henschel Hs 126 reconnaissance aircraft to safety. Just over 600 of these aircraft were built but they were progressively replaced from 1942 by the twin-engined Focke-Wulf Fw 189.

Soviet anti-aircraft gunners prepare to defend Kharkov against air attack. The liberation of the city lasted just a month.

The Red Army's T-34 tanks rolled triumphantly into Dzerzhinsky Square in mid-February 1943 following Field Marshal von Manstein's evacuation of the city.

These ski troops are armed with the Soviet PPSh 41 submachine gun. At first glance they look like Russians but they are actually German. These men conducted deep penetration reconnaissance missions in advance of their tanks. The Soviet PPSh family of submachine guns were cheap and cheerful, simple to manufacture, used pistol ammunition (which was cheaper to produce than rifle ammunition) and required little training. The PPSh, along with the Model 1940 steel helmet, came to epitomise the image of the Soviet infantryman, especially during the brutal street fighting throughout the Soviet Union.

A German gunner mans a defensive position. Having evacuated Kharkov, the Germans were able to hold the Red Army to the west of the city.

This German bunker is defended by a captured Russian Maxim heavy machine gun.

A German soldier emerges from his bunker ready to engage advancing Soviet infantry.

A Soviet prisoner of war wearing a *budenovka* cloth helmet to keep out the cold. While preferable to the M1940 steel helmet or the cloth side cap, the *budenovka* was not as warm as the *ushanka* fur cap. Having evacuated Kharkov, Manstein was able to attack the Soviet salient protruding towards Dnepropetrovsk.

Two tough-looking German soldiers watching an air attack or artillery bombardment on Soviet positions. The reversible camouflage/white special winter combat uniform was introduced in time for the second Russian winter of the war. It consisted of hood, coat, trousers, mittens and special underwear. The first pattern had field grey on one side and white on the other, the second geometric camouflage and the third mottled camouflage. The boots were made of felt with leather soles and binding. These uniforms made the winter of 1942/3 far more bearable than the previous one.

SS Panzer IVs re-entering Kharkov. The defeat of Rybalko's 3rd Tank Army had left the city open to recapture.

A German Marder self-propelled gun prepares for action. Having defeated the Red Army between the Dnieper and the Don, Manstein counterattacked towards Kharkov with the I SS Panzer Corps swinging to the east.

Once again Kharkov suffered as the Red Army fought its way back to the Donets.

An SS Sd Kfz 251 semi-tracked armoured personnel carrier on the streets of Kharkov. The inhabitants were dismayed to find their liberation so short-lived and the Germans were swift to reassert control.

An honour guard saluting the dead. The SS Panzer Corps lost 11,000 casualties in all. Of these, some 4,500 were lost by the 1st SS Panzer Division in recapturing Kharkov.

Once more Kharkov proved to be a terrible killing ground for the Red Army. During Manstein's Kharkov riposte in the second week of March 1943, the Germans claimed to have killed 50,000 Soviet troops and captured 19,500. For Stalin and his generals it must have felt like May 1942 all over again.

Chapter Seven

Final Battle for Kharkov – August 1943

Just after Hitler's calamitous defeat at Kursk, a fourth and final battle was fought for Kharkov between 12 and 23 August 1943. The panzers did all they could to halt the Soviet attack and inflicted huge losses, but the Germans' lack of manpower and critical shortages of ammunition meant there could only be one outcome. Following Hitler's failed attempt to cut off the Kursk salient, Zhukov unleashed his massive Soviet counteroffensive, sweeping back the Germans' hard-won gains and pushing them out of their Orel and Kharkov salients to the north and south of the Kursk bulge. The first Operation Kutuzov, the Orel strategic counteroffensive, ran from 12 July to 18 August 1942 and was designed to destroy the German Army's positions at Orel.

This capitalised on the Wehrmacht's shortcomings and further emphasised that the strategic and operational initiative had passed over to the Red Army and the Red Air Force. The Soviets intended not only to liberate the salient, but also to ensnare as much as possible of General Walther Model's 2nd Panzer Army (its previous commander, Rudolf Schmidt, had been sacked on 11 July) and the 9th Army also commanded by Model, both of which formed part of Kluge's Army Group Centre.

The Soviets launched their attack with the relative fresh forces of General V.D. Sokolovsky's West Front and General M.M. Popov's Bryansk Front, neither of which had been directly involved in the Kursk fighting. It was intended that the West Front's 3rd and 63rd Armies would push west from the Novosil area over the Susha river, cutting through the junction of the 2nd Panzer Army and the 9th Army to liberate Orel. This would pin the Germans down while the 3rd Guards Tank Army pushed its armour through to exploit the situation further west. In the meantime the West Front's 11th Guards Army was to attack south from the Belev area to smash the left shoulder of the German salient, which would allow the 4th Tank Army to press on and cut off the 2nd Panzer Army, ensuring the destruction of its armoured forces.

Model and Kluge were not ignorant of Soviet intentions; photoreconnaissance and radio intercepts provided a clear picture of what the Red Army intended. Model simply did not have sufficient manpower to conduct any spoiling attacks, but this intelligence did at least enable his men to prepare in-depth defences. This was especially important for General Dr Rendulic's 35th Corps, which would bear the brunt of the 63rd Army's attack. In the event, the latter was only able to make slow progress towards Orel. To the north the 11th Guards Army pushed the Germans back 16 miles in two days in the face of bitter resistance.

Operation Kutuzov overlapped with Operation Polkovodets Rumyantsev, the Belgorod–Kharkov strategic offensive, from 3 to 23 August 1943. This was the Red Army's counteroffensive against the southern sector of the Kursk bulge, following Hitler's Operation Citadel. The Soviet Steppe Front committed four armies, comprising the 7th Guards, 57th, 69th and 5th Tank Armies, supported by 800 tanks. This force was to push back Manstein's Army Group South with the aim of liberating both Belgorod and Kharkov.

On the night of 5/6 August General Erhard Raus' 11th Corps (little more than an ad hoc battle group drawn from five different infantry divisions) evacuated Belgorod and took up positions between the Donets and Lopan rivers north of Kharkov. These positions were, however, compromised by Soviet forces up to 20 miles behind them and the 11th Corps was forced to withdraw towards Kharkov, which it reached on the 12th, having successfully conducted a rearguard action to the Donets.

The Soviet Air Force also played a role in the Wehrmacht's defeat. Large numbers of bombers hit German rear areas, targeting airfields, roads and railways as well as supplies and reserves struggling to reach the front. Anything that moved was bombed and strafed. To try to prevent the panzers moving forwards to bolster the inadequate defences at Kharkov, Soviet bombers conducted 2,300 sorties against trains and railway stations between 6 and 17 August 1943. Close air support missions accounted for up to 80 per cent of the daily sorties. The German Army was used to seeing the Luftwaffe thumping the Red Army; now the tables had been turned.

As soon as Soviet troops cut the Poltava–Kharkov rail link, General Raus' position at Kharkov would be seriously jeopardised. Despite the presence of large numbers of administrative and logistical personnel in the city, the 11th Corps could muster only 4,000 infantrymen. In addition, ammunition stocks were precariously low. The intense fighting in the Battle of Kursk had consumed half of the ammunition that had been set aside for the end of August and early September. As a result, the supply depot in Kharkov had five trainloads of spare panzer tracks but not much else.

On 12 August General Werner Kempf, commanding Army Detachment Kempf, requested permission to abandon Kharkov and Manstein agreed but Hitler insisted the city be held. Kempf was replaced with General Otto Wöhler and his former command became the German 8th Army. Hitler was worried that the loss of Kharkov would damage his prestige with Turkey, which although officially neutral was pro-Nazi. In the spring the Turkish commander-in-chief had inspected Kempf's defences and pronounced them 'impregnable'. Kharkov was also on the long list of towns and cities that Hitler had decreed should be held to the last man – thereby shackling the Wehrmacht to innumerable costly defensive battles and depriving them of the initiative.

The mood in General Raus' headquarters cannot have been a happy one, but German generals had found themselves in this type of situation on innumerable occasions and had still turned the tables on the enemy. Raus was actually Austrian, but he was an experienced leader, having commanded the 6th Panzer Division during the early part of the war.

Examining his maps, Raus anticipated that the Red Army would attempt to cut off Kharkov by breaking through the defensive arc to the west of the city. He therefore rushed every anti-tank gun and 88mm flak gun to the high ground on the northern edge of the precarious bottleneck, which would have to be kept open to facilitate an escape route for withdrawing units. Despite the efforts of the Red Air Force, these defences were further reinforced by the welcome and timely arrival of panzers from the 2nd SS Panzer Division, giving Raus 96 Panthers, 35 Tigers and 25 Sturmgeschütz III assault guns. These were capable of giving Soviet tanks a very bloody nose.

As the Red Army began to mass for its attack on 20 August, its units were promptly set upon by the Luftwaffe's Stuka dive-bombers. Raus recalled: 'Dark fountains of earth erupted skyward and were followed by heavy thunderclaps and shocks that resembled an earthquake. These were the heaviest, 2-ton, bombs, designed for use against battleships, which were all that Luftflotte 4 had left to counter the Russian attack. Soon all the villages occupied by Soviet tanks lay in flames.'

Soviet tanks advanced through the broad cornfields, emerging on the east–west highway several hundred metres from Raus' main defences. Initially the Panthers held the T-34s at bay, but sheer weight of numbers brought them to the German forward battle positions. 'Here a net of anti-tank and flak guns, Hornet 88mm tank destroyers, and Wasp self-propelled 105mm field howitzers trapped the T-34s, split them into small groups, and put large numbers out of action,' recalled Raus. 'The final waves were still attempting to force a breakthrough in concentrated masses when Tigers and StuG III self-propelled assault guns, which represented our mobile reserves behind the front, attacked the Russian armour and repulsed it with heavy losses.' The 5th Guards Tank Army lost 184 T-34s that day. In total, the Red Army lost 450 tanks during the Belgorod–Kharkov offensive.

Although the Luftwaffe and the panzers had done all they could to halt the Soviets, with their ammunition and strength spent there was little more they could do. Insisting that the garrison remain at their posts was simply a waste of valuable manpower. On 21 August 1943 Manstein abandoned the battered city of Kharkov for the second time, and two days later the Red Army was in the city centre once more. The retreating Germans blew up their remaining ammunition and fuel dumps and set fire to parts of the city to slow down the advancing enemy. To the south of Kharkov the German rearguard fought desperately to hold open the escape corridor as troop convoys sped to safety. Eventually Raus and his 11th Corps, despite repeated Soviet attacks and attempts to cut them off, fought their way back to the Dnieper.

When Soviet aerial reconnaissance spotted the Germans withdrawing from Kharkov towards Poltava, the air force flew 1,300 sorties against the retreating columns. The roads soon became choked with blazing vehicles. Following the evacuation of Kharkov's surrounding airfields on 23 August, most of the Luftwaffe units withdrew to bases near Dnepropetrovsk, Kremenchug and Mirogorod to help defend the Dnieper line. This was driven by Hitler's desire to hold the Crimea, but at the same time exposed the northern flank of the Ukrainian salient. This weakness soon became apparent to Soviet aerial reconnaissance.

Early in the morning on 23 August elements of the Soviet 183rd Rifle Division triumphantly reached Kharkov's Dzerzhinsky Square, where they linked up with soldiers from the 89th Rifle Division and hoisted the Red Banner over the ruins. The city was completely liberated by 11am and the fourth and final battle for Kharkov was over. The success of this operation meant that German forces in Ukraine were forced to withdraw behind the Dnieper and this paved the way for the liberation of Kiev in early November.

At the end of July events in Italy took a hand as the Italian dictator Benito Mussolini was ousted, following the Western Allies' landing on Sicily. Field Marshal von Kluge was ordered to evacuate the Orel salient. Despite the committal of the Soviet Central Front on the southern shoulder of the salient, the Germans were able to withdraw to the half-completed Hagen Line in front of Bryansk. There was to be little respite for them, however, for on 23 August Zhukov launched an offensive to push the Germans back from Nevel south to the Black Sea, defended by Army Groups Centre, South and A.

The Soviet victory came at a terrible price. Losses for the three Soviet Fronts totalled 177,847 men and 1,614 tanks and self-propelled guns. German losses were just short of 50,000 men (Army Group South 29,102 and 9th Army 20,720), while

1,612 panzers were damaged, only 323 of which were beyond repair. The Germans also lost Belgorod and Kharkov. From this point on Hitler, like it or not, was on the strategic defensive on the Eastern Front.

Fearful of being outflanked, the bulk of the German forces in the Soviet Union fell back on the Dnieper river. To the west of Moscow the Red Army, from early August to the beginning of October, struggled in a series of operations to push back the Wehrmacht and liberate Smolensk. These operations were conducted by the Kalinin and Western Fronts against Army Group Centre. Smolensk was liberated in late September at the cost of 450,000 Soviet casualties; German losses were assessed at around a quarter of a million. This finally removed the strategic threat to Moscow.

The heavy losses suffered by the Wehrmacht in July and August 1943 crippled both Army Groups Centre and South. Notably, for the first time the Germans were unable to defeat a major Soviet summer offensive (the Polkovodets Rumyantsev and the concurrent Kutuzov operations). Manstein was unable to launch another Kharkov comeback and the Red Army's momentum of 1943 was to continue unabated in 1944, with catastrophic consequences for Hitler.

Battle-hardened German officers and NCOs taking a rest and enjoying the sunshine. The lack of helmets indicates they are a safe distance from the fighting. In the summer of 1943 everything hung on Hitler's massive knock-out blow by Army Groups Centre and South against the Red Army's exposed salient at Kursk.

Operation Citadel – Hitler's assault at Kursk – set great store by the powerful Tiger tank, seen here undergoing field maintenance with a special crane, and the Panther tank. It was hoped that their superior firepower and gunnery would chew up the Soviet T-34s with decisive results – but this was proved wrong. Tigers were also used in the defence of Kharkov in late August 1943.

Apprehensive-looking German infantry getting ready to go into battle. Their rather scruffy appearance shows they have been in the line for some time. The fourth man from the left appears to be listening to something – perhaps a preliminary artillery or Luftwaffe bombardment.

German troops watching the panzers going in. Kursk was an all-or-nothing gamble.

This soldier's expression of deep concern says it all: the defeat at Kursk meant the armies in the surrounding areas were at risk. The German MP38 and MP40 submachine guns were highly crafted weapons but were never issued in significant numbers.

His comrades lay Hans Beyer to rest. Between 5 and 20 July 1943 the Germans lost almost 50,000 men in the Battle of Kursk, while the Red Army lost almost 178,000.

The remains of a Soviet STZ-5-2TB tracked prime mover used to tow artillery. The Germans employed captured examples as the Artillerie Schlepper CT3-601(r).

Under German guard, Soviet prisoners add more dead to an existing graveyard.

These men do not appear to appreciate having their photo taken, greeting the camera with a mixture of hostility and indifference. Both look noticeably tired. After Operation Citadel was brought to a halt, the Red Army launched a massive counteroffensive. The Germans had to conduct a fighting retreat as they were driven from the Orel and Kharkov salients to the north and south of the Kursk bulge.

In the face of the Soviet Belgorod–Kharkov offensive, General Raus' 11th Corps, drawn from elements of five infantry divisions, was forced to evacuate Belgorod and withdraw on Kharkov in early August 1943. Whether trudging along on foot or in motor vehicles, they inevitably attracted the attention of the Red Air Force.

Another German machine-gun position concealed to catch unwary Soviet infantry. General Raus appreciated that Soviet tanks would try to cut off his garrison by sweeping to the west of the city, so bolstered his defences to the north.

This gunner outside his log bunker is armed with the MG34. Kharkov was surrounded by a belt of defensive positions such as this.

German engineers laying field telephone cables take a rest in a roadside ditch. Such phone lines were easily cut by artillery fire.

German officers snatch a quick meal; the drivers loiter nervously with their vehicles on the nearby road. The fighting was so fluid that it was easy to end up behind enemy lines.

In defence of Kharkov General Raus was able to muster just 4,000 infantrymen and 156 tanks with which to fend off the Soviet 5th Guards Tank Army. It was a thankless and hopeless task but Hitler insisted the city be held.

Red Army shelling and attacks by the Red Air Force greatly hampered the German defence of Kharkov. Passing Germans pause to watch a burning building.

When Manstein ordered Kharkov be abandoned to the Red Army on 21 August 1943, the retreating Wehrmacht set fire to parts of the city and blew up supply dumps to slow the enemy's advance.

This is what greeted the liberators of Kharkov: malnourished orphans and starving women.

Civilians hurry past war-damaged buildings near Kharkov's Assumption Cathedral. The sedan in the background may be carrying Soviet military officials. It would be a long time before the city could return to any sort of normality.

The Germans soon found themselves withdrawing over great distances as they tried to establish new defensive lines. This process was greatly hampered once the rains set in and the muddy season started.

Soviet dead gathered up by local peasants for burial. Soviet losses were enormous but after the victory at Kursk and the liberation of Kharkov, final victory for Stalin began to look more assured. Stalin could afford to trade bodies, but the Wehrmacht, facing an increasing manpower shortage, could not.

A German funeral party fires a salute over fallen comrades. Trying to fend off the Red Army's Belgorod–Kharkov offensive cost Army Group South thousands of casualties.

Chapter Eight

The Aftermath

The Red Army's victory at Kharkov in the summer of 1943 meant that it had firmly avenged the disaster at Barenkovo the previous year. From 20 October the Luftwaffe concentrated its efforts for about a week on the Red Army advancing from Kremenchug on the Dnieper towards Krivoi Rog. This helped the German Army halt the Soviet advance short of Krivoi Rog. However, this success came at a price. The concentration of units greatly weakened the Luftwaffe between Kiev and the Pripet Marshes, and that, along with the Army's shift southwards, left the way open for the liberation of Kiev.

Soviet forces rolled back into the Ukrainian capital on 6 November 1943. By December the Red Army had advanced up to 800 miles and liberated almost two-thirds of the territory conquered by the Wehrmacht. The liberation of Kiev and the consolidation of sizeable bridgeheads over the Dnieper further south, less than five months after Hitler had thrown everything at Kursk, clearly illustrated what combined Soviet air–land power was capable of achieving over vast distances when given the right resources and leadership.

At the end of the year Stalin sought to liberate Ukraine west of the Dnieper. The 1st, 2nd, 3rd and 4th Ukrainian Fronts massed 2.3 million men, 2,040 tanks and self-propelled guns, 28,800 field guns and mortars and 2,370 aircraft to smash Manstein's Army Group South and Kleist's Army Group A. The Germans could muster 1.7 million troops, with 2,200 panzers, 16,800 field guns and 1,460 aircraft. In addition, 50,000 Soviet partisans played a role in disrupting German rear areas.

In the wake of the Germans taking Zhitomir and their attempts on Kiev, the Soviet high command ordered the 1st Ukrainian Front to destroy the 4th Panzer Army in the Zhitomir–Berdichev Operation. For the attack Vatutin's 1st Ukrainian Front massed sixty-three infantry divisions and three cavalry divisions, plus six tank corps and two mechanised corps.

The offensive commenced on 24 December 1943 and within six days had forced a breakthrough 187 miles wide and 62 miles deep. The breach southwest of Kiev drove the 4th Panzer Army back over 100 miles, exposing the German 8th Army's right flank and its foothold on the southern banks of the Dnieper, and it was not long before the Red Army was attempting to ensnare it. This was vital as these forces sat astride the junction of the 1st and 2nd Ukrainian Fronts.

It was called the Korsun–Shevchenkovsky salient by the Soviets, but is also known as the Cherkassy pocket. According to Soviet intelligence, the 1st Panzer and 8th Armies had nine infantry, one panzer and one motorised division in the salient. To overwhelm them, on 24 January 1944 the Red Army launched twenty-seven rifle divisions, four tank corps, one mechanised corps and one cavalry corps armed with 370 tanks and self-propelled guns and almost 4,000 guns and mortars.

The German high command ordered a counter-attack, with the 3rd, 4th, 11th and 13th Panzer Divisions sent to the Novo-Mirgorod region. The 16th and 7th Panzer Divisions were also gathered in the Rizino area. However, the Red Army's second envelopment attempt on 3 February succeeded when the 1st and 2nd Ukrainian Fronts linked up near Zvenigorodka, trapping 56,000 Germans in the Cherkassy pocket.

Desperately the Germans attempted a two-pronged relief, with the 1st Panzer Army's 3rd Panzer Corps driving from the southwest and the 8th Army's 47th Panzer Corps striking from the south. The 5th SS Panzer Division led the breakout on 16 February, only to be met by the Soviet 4th Guards and 27th Armies. The Soviets claimed the battle resulted in 55,000 German dead or wounded and 18,200 prisoners, while the Germans maintained that 30,000 men escaped, with 20,000 killed and 8,000 captured.

After Vatutin was mortally wounded, Zhukov took charge of destroying Manstein's Army Group South, aiming to trap the 1st Panzer and 4th Panzer Armies along with 200,000 men. He attacked on 4 March, covering 100 miles in just a few days. Once the 1st Ukrainian Front reached the Tarnopol–Proskurov line and the 2nd Ukrainian Front cleared Uman and forced the Southern Bug near Dzhulinka, the 1st Panzer Army was indeed threatened with encirclement. On the route to Uman the Germans lost 200 panzers, 600 field guns and 12,000 lorries as they sought to flee. The Red Army had avenged the humiliation of the Uman pocket in 1941.

In the Crimea General Erwin Jänecke's 17th Army, cut off since the end of 1943 by the 4th Ukrainian and North Caucasian Fronts, faced a similar fate to that of the 6th Army at Stalingrad. Although protected by considerable defences, the situation for the German and Romanian defenders, totalling around 230,000 men, with 215 panzers, 3,600 guns and mortars and 148 aircraft, was not good. The 4th Ukrainian Front attacking from the north and the Separate Maritime Army from the east had an overwhelming strength of 470,000 men, 559 tanks and self-propelled guns, and nearly 6,000 field guns and mortars, all supported by 1,250 aircraft.

The Red Army's offensive to liberate the Crimea commenced in earnest on 8 April. The fall of Kerch three days later sealed the fate of the defenders and once it became apparent that the northern Perekop defences could not hold, the Germans began to evacuate regardless of Hitler's orders to stand fast. Up until mid-May the Romanian Navy evacuated almost 121,000 men across the Black Sea. Pushed back to Sevastopol, the Germans lost 12,221 men and the Romanians 17,652, plus nearly all their armour. The 17th Army held until 9 May and the Khersones bridgehead lasted until the 12th, when the last 3,000 troops were overwhelmed. In total, some 25,000 German troops surrendered that day.

From December 1943 to May 1944 the Red Army expelled the Wehrmacht from most of Ukraine. Similarly, from January to March 1944 the Red Army drove the Germans steadily away from Leningrad and Novgorod. Hitler and his generals were anticipating a Soviet summer offensive but they had no way of appreciating its vast scale. Thanks to Soviet deception efforts, Hitler anticipated another assault on Army Group North Ukraine and diverted increasingly scarce resources there. Instead, Stalin sought to liberate Byelorussia and its capital Minsk with his version of D-Day.

Hitler's victories around Kharkov during 1941–1943 ensured that he maintained control of Ukraine. In 1941 the Red Army simply did not have the resources to hold Kharkov. Efforts in 1942 and 1943 to liberate the city proved ill-conceived when on both occasions the Soviets were outmastered by vastly superior German generalship. The May 1942 defeat was a particular humiliation and could have been avoided if Stalin had permitted Timoshenko to safeguard his southern flank or withdraw back across the Dnieper once the German counterattack started.

Of all the battles fought around Kharkov it is Field Marshal von Manstein's masterstroke in March 1943 that showed what could be achieved if the leaden hand of Hitler was lifted. On this occasion giving ground produced quite remarkable results and held off defeat in Ukraine for another five months. Only in the wake of Hitler's crushing defeat at Kursk was Stalin able to press home and finally liberate the city once and for all.

In a snapshot for a loved one, this Red Army NCO is wearing the traditional style Russian cut shirt with stand collar. This was reintroduced in 1943 for wear with shoulder boards in order to make military rank clearer. The reintroduction of Tsarist ranks may in part have been responsible for helping to invigorate the Soviet military.

Red Army dead lay strewn at the roadside as a German column rumbles by. Soviet troops suffered heavy casualties throughout the summer of 1943, but the sacrifice eventually achieved victory with the Germans driven from Ukraine.

These prisoners of war are wearing the standard Red Army uniform of khaki field tunic and breeches plus standard issue knee-length leather boots. In 1943 the shirt in traditional Russian style with stand collar and no breast pockets was reintroduced for wear with shoulder boards. This was issued in olive green but soon faded to a sand colour.

A German corporal and his comrade pose with a looted Soviet banner. Had they been captured with it, they would have suffered a hefty beating or worse.

More German fatalities interred by their mourning comrades. After the liberation of Kharkov some 20,000 German troops were killed in the Cherkassy pocket.

This decapitated statue of Stalin was a stark reminder of the presence of occupying forces.

The German occupation of the Soviet Union resulted in the wholesale destruction of cities in Russia, Byelorussia and Ukraine. Historic buildings and monuments were laid waste by the fighting and wanton vandalism.

An early model T-26 light tank lies abandoned on the streets in silent testimony to the Wehrmacht's earlier victories in 1941.

A soldier examining captured Soviet weapons.

Kiev, the Ukrainian capital, was liberated on 6 November 1943. The Germans blew up everything they could not take with them, including what remained of the city's factories.

Through the winter of 1943/44 German forces were expelled from the Crimea and Ukraine by a series of Red Army offensives.

Another Maxim machine gun and some M40 helmets mark German war graves. At Sevastopol in the Crimea the Germans lost over 12,000 dead and 25,000 men captured.

Initially many Ukrainians welcomed the German invasion in the hope that Hitler would support Ukrainian nationalism. In reality, Hitler had little interest in supporting such aspirations. Occupying forces made only half-hearted attempts to court local politicians and Ukrainian recruits were relegated to security operations.

A Luftwaffe officer accosts a local in front of a toppled statue of Stalin. The liberation of Kharkov and then Kiev in 1943 marked the expulsion of the Wehrmacht from Ukraine. Byelorussia and Minsk would follow suit in the summer of 1944.

The mud always hampered movement more than the snow and ice on the Eastern Front. Evacuating occupied towns and villages became a major logistical exercise, which was given greater impetus as the front lines drew ever closer to the rear echelon units.

This soldier pays his respects to Corporal Benz, who was killed on 28 March 1943. As the Germans withdrew they had no way of repatriating those buried in the Soviet Union. Inevitably tens of thousands of graves were despoiled by the vengeful Red Army.

As the Germans were driven back through December 1943 to May 1944 graves became once again increasingly makeshift.

Ukrainian civilians return to their homes in the wake of the Red Army's hard-won victories.